# Exploring the Basic Income Guarantee

Series Editor
Karl Widerquist, Georgetown University in Qatar, Doha, USA

Basic income is one of the most innovative, powerful, straightforward, and controversial proposals for addressing poverty and growing inequalities. A Basic Income Guarantee (BIG) is designed to be an unconditional, government-insured guarantee that all citizens will have enough income to meet their basic needs. The concept of basic, or guaranteed, income is a form of social provision and this series examines the arguments for and against it from an interdisciplinary perspective with special focus on the economic and social factors. By systematically connecting abstract philosophical debates over competing principles of BIG to the empirical analysis of concrete policy proposals, this series contributes to the fields of economics, politics, social policy, and philosophy and establishes a theoretical framework for interdisciplinary research. It will bring together international and national scholars and activists to provide a comparative look at the main efforts to date to pass unconditional BIG legislation across regions of the globe and will identify commonalities and differences across countries drawing lessons for advancing social policies in general and BIG policies in particular.

Simon Watkins

# Basic Income, Work Incentives and Job Search Behaviour

## Bridging Theory and Practice in European Contexts

palgrave
macmillan

Simon Watkins
Holt, Wiltshire, UK

ISSN 2662-3803 ISSN 2662-3811 (electronic)
Exploring the Basic Income Guarantee
ISBN 978-3-031-99196-7 ISBN 978-3-031-99197-4 (eBook)
https://doi.org/10.1007/978-3-031-99197-4



This Palgrave Macmillan imprint is published by the registered company Springer Nature Switzerland AG
The registered company address is: Gewerbestrasse 11, 6330 Cham, Switzerland

*Acknowledgements* Many things have happened since I started a PhD research project which has now been adapted into a book. The most significant being a global pandemic, marriage and relocating with my family. There have been periods when not much progress was made, and many times when I thought of giving up. The fact that I didn't is testament to the following people.

I cannot imagine having achieved this without the help of my PhD supervisors, Professor Nigel Gilbert and Dr. Corinna Elsenbroich, who have supported me since the beginning. Both went above and beyond in helping me to complete the thesis, through the pandemic and out the other side. Dr. Kavin Narasimhan and Dr. Jill Timms joined the team towards the end, just as things were ramping up, and were a source of great help and advice.

Special thanks to my wife, Jo, for providing endless amounts of love, support and cups of tea. Thanks also to my son, Elliott, for giving me perspective when it was hard to find, and to my two step-sons, Leo and Jude. Thanks to my parents for babysitting in the early years so I could escape to the library for a few hours, and for their love and support too. Thanks also to Paola, for not letting me give up, even when I really wanted to.

*Competing Interests* The author has no competing interests to declare that are relevant to the content of this manuscript.

# Contents

# List of Figures

# List of Tables

CHAPTER 1

# Rethinking Basic Income: Welfare Principles, Institutional Contexts, and Job Search Behaviour

**Abstract** This book examines how basic income may impact on job search behaviour amongst unemployed individuals by analysing its defining principles, unconditionality, universalism, and non-withdrawal, within existing welfare regimes. The research develops a new ideal type framework to measure how closely ten European welfare regimes approximate basic income principles. Using qualitative comparative analysis and time use data, the study examines a range of welfare configurations to identify their impact on job search intensity. The findings challenge conventional assumptions about basic income's incentivising effects, revealing that its impact is neither linear nor deterministic but emerges from complex interactions between policy mechanisms and institutional contexts. This approach provides a foundation for more realistic expectations about basic income implementation and advances debates that have often relied more on theoretical assumptions than systematic evidence.

**Keywords** Basic income principles · Job search behaviour · Welfare regimes · Labour market participation · Qualitative comparative analysis (QCA) · Unconditionality · Universalism



S. Watkins, *Basic Income, Work Incentives and Job Search Behaviour*, Exploring the Basic Income Guarantee,
https://doi.org/10.1007/978-3-031-99197-4_1

Debates around the efficacy of basic income, a regular cash payment made to every individual without means-test or work requirement, have grown and matured over recent years. At the same time, the idea of a basic income has gained mainstream traction, no longer confined to the margins of welfare debates. It has emerged as a potential policy response to evolving economic and social realities, and increasingly so as technological change reshapes employment patterns and precarious work becomes more prevalent.

However, a fundamental question remains: how would basic income affect people's relationship with paid work, particularly their motivations to seek and retain employment? In the absence of definitive data from a fully implemented basic income policy, this question has until now been approached through two methods. Firstly, a growing number of basic income experiments, from experiments in the United States and Canada in the 1960s and 1970s, to more recent studies in India, Africa, Europe, and North American contexts. Whilst these experiments offer valuable insights, they are limited by their temporary nature, specific local contexts, and methodological constraints. The second approach relies on theoretical arguments about human behaviour in response to economic incentives, often supported by limited empirical evidence.

This book addresses the critical question of basic income's potential effect on work motivations, focusing specifically on its potential impact on job search behaviours amongst unemployed people. However, its approach differs from previous examinations of the question. Instead of treating basic income as a single policy intervention, it examines three mechanisms that define basic income: unconditionality, universalism, and non-withdrawal. These mechanisms are already present to varying degrees in existing welfare regimes, creating natural laboratories for understanding their effects on job search behaviour. Through analysis and discussion of the complex relationships between basic income mechanisms, this book introduces a new way of thinking about basic income, not just as policy but as a set of ideal types of welfare regime characteristics, creating a framework for measuring how closely existing welfare regimes approximate basic income principles. This approach enables the research within this book to examine how different combinations of welfare mechanisms affect job search behaviours. It also enables the identification of institutional factors that may increase or decrease the impact of basic income and allows evidence based predictions about basic income's potential effects across different welfare regimes to be made.

In this sense, this book deepens our understanding of how existing welfare regimes differ from basic income through the development of a new conceptual framework: an ideal type welfare regime. Using set theoretic methods, it examines key principles underpinning the idea of basic income, specifically unconditionality, universality, and non-withdrawable payments, to assess the extent of alignment or deviation across welfare systems. It also fills a gap in existing welfare literature by highlighting the specific characteristics that make some countries more akin to a basic income than others.

## Normative Perspectives on Labour Market Reductions

Examining basic income's potential effects on job search behaviour and labour market participation highlights a fundamental normative debate on work ethics: whether potential reductions in paid work would be beneficial or harmful. This debate reflects broader philosophical perspectives on the role of work in society but is often overlooked when discussing the potential effects of basic income. Critics of basic income often frame decreased labour market participation as inherently problematic, potentially undermining economic productivity, tax revenues, and social integration through work (Minogue, 2018; White, 2023). It is notable that such arguments are commonly based on theoretical arguments unsupported by empirical evidence. From this perspective, any policy that might reduce work effort represents a fundamental flaw. However, many basic income advocates argue that moderate reductions in paid work are actually desirable for a number of reasons. Modest work reductions might enable people to pursue education, care responsibilities, community engagement, entrepreneurship, or creative pursuits that are valuable but not well-compensated by markets (Raventós, 2007; Swaine, 2011; Van Parijs, 1992, 2017). Such reductions could represent enhanced freedom rather than dependency, allowing individuals to allocate time according to their values rather than purely economic necessity (Widerquist & Lewis, 2006).

Job search intensity, defined as the time and effort individuals devote to finding employment (Benhabib & Bull, 1983; Bloemen, 2005; Faberman & Kudlyak, 2014, 2019Krueger & Mueller, 2012), and measured in this book based on time use data, serves as an important indicator of labour market participation. Understanding how basic income may affect job search intensity is important as it helps us to understand how basic income functions as an incentive or disincentive to find work, a crucial indicator of labour market participation. Exploring the potential impact of basic income on job search behaviour and labour market participation more broadly are central to it moving from theory to practice.

Throughout this book, two related but distinct terms are used to discuss how unemployed people look for work. 'Job search activity' refers to the broader concept and qualitative aspects of job searching behaviours across different welfare regimes. 'Job search intensity' refers specifically to the quantitative measure developed in Chapter 7 that combines both participation rate (whether people engage in job search) and participation time (how much time they spend on it). This distinction allows for greater precision when discussing both the general concept and the specific measurement approach.

This book examines job search behaviour as an empirical question without presuming that increased or decreased work effort is inherently preferable. Whilst acknowledging that paid work remains central to financial security and societal organisation, the analysis recognises the legitimacy of different normative perspectives on how work should be distributed and valued in society. The findings thus serve both those concerned about potential work disincentives and those interested in basic income's capacity to enhance freedom and wellbeing through greater individual autonomy over work decisions.

In advancing debates on basic income, this book critically examines the often-overlooked contradictory incentives and disincentives embedded in basic income mechanisms. Drawing on empirical evidence from a range of existing welfare regimes, it explores whether these mechanisms, individually or in combination, affect job search activity. It is the first study to do so. It applies counterfactual analysis to conduct a thought experiment, assessing the potential impact of basic income within various institutional contexts. This innovative approach extends existing knowledge by exploring hypothetical policy outcomes. The study challenges the widely held assumption that basic income necessarily incentivises employment through reductions in effective tax rates when moving from unemployment into work. It finds no evidence of such effects in countries exhibiting basic income like mechanisms.

## Contradictory Work Incentives

Basic income presents something of a paradox when thinking about incentivising job search behaviour. Its unconditionality removes the requirement to actively search for a job. This has been cast as a disincentive to find work. However, its non-withdrawal and not being means-tested represent an increased financial incentive to work, as people will be better off working than not working. Meanwhile, its universal nature may act as a disincentive to work as eligibility for payments is not dependent on previous or ongoing work record, as is the case with many existing benefits. These contradictory mechanisms make it difficult to predict what basic income's overall impact may be in relation to job search behaviour and labour market participation more broadly. Previous research has typically focused on individual mechanisms in isolation, missing the potential interactive effects, as well as the role of institutional context in shaping outcomes.

## A New Analytical Framework

This book develops an innovative approach to analysing and understanding the complex relationships between basic income mechanisms. It conceptualises basic income's defining features as ideal types of welfare regime characteristics, creating a framework for measuring how closely existing welfare regimes approximate basic income principles. This approach enables the research to examine how different combinations of welfare mechanisms affect job search behaviours. It also enables the identification of institutional factors that may increase or decrease the impact of basic income and allows evidence based predictions about basic income's potential effects across different welfare regimes to be made.

This book advances understanding of the degree to which existing welfare regimes differ from basic income through the development of a new conceptual framework, an ideal type welfare regime, based on set theoretic methods which examine key principles which underpin the idea of basic income, specifically unconditionality, universality, and non-withdrawable payments. It fills a gap in existing welfare literature by highlighting the specific characteristics that make some countries more akin to a basic income than others. To this end, the analysis identifies which existing welfare regimes most closely resemble a basic income welfare regime. It then explores what different configurations of welfare mechanisms result in varying degrees of job search activity amongst unemployed people. Drawing inferences from the analysis, it provides a better understanding of the potential effects of a basic income on job search activities of unemployed people.

## Research Aims and Methodology

This book examines the potential impact of basic income on job search activities amongst unemployed people in a variety of institutional and cultural contexts. To do this it undertakes the following elements of research:

1. It develops an ideal type framework, based on the main principles of basic income, and uses the framework to measure the unemployment benefits across ten European countries to determine which countries' welfare regimes most resemble an ideal type basic income.
2. It then develops a measure of job search intensity to determine which countries have high levels of job search intensity amongst unemployed people and which have low job search intensity.
3. It undertakes analysis to determine what conditions are necessary and sufficient for the presence of high levels or low levels of job search activity amongst unemployed people.
4. Based on the findings of the research, it synthesises existing research and the research in this book to examine the likely effects of basic income on job search activity amongst unemployed people.

The analysis focuses on ten European countries, chosen purposely as representatives of a range of welfare regimes, but also due to the limitations of the availability of specific data, namely the 2010 round of the Harmonised European Time Use Data Surveys, on which the measure of job search intensity is built.

The research uses set theoretic methods (Duşa, 2020), specifically two elements of qualitative comparative analysis, fuzzy set ideal type analysis and fuzzy set qualitative comparative analysis, to firstly develop the basic income ideal type welfare regime, then measure job search intensity, and finally to uncover the necessary and sufficient conditions for the presence of high and low job search intensity amongst unemployed people across European countries. It therefore represents a new avenue of investigation in the basic income debate, examining the outcome of a non-existent combination of attributes, based on counterfactual analysis, to provide a better understanding of the potential effects of a basic income on job search activities of unemployed people, set within existing national contexts of European countries.

## Empirical Scope of the Book

The empirical scope of this book extends to ten European countries at a specific point in time. The countries included have been chosen as they represent a range of approaches to welfare provision and have been previously categorised as types of different welfare regimes. The specific years chosen are due to data considerations, as they correlate to the availability of time use data, which is used to develop the measure of job search activity, which serves as the outcome in the analysis. The countries and years are set out in Table 1.1.

The book builds on the extensive literature on ideal type welfare regimes, including Esping-Andersen's seminal work on identifying distinct constellations of welfare regimes (Wilensky, 1974; Titmuss, 1974; Esping-Andersen, 1990, 1999; Ferrera, 1996; Leibfried, 2002; Bambra, 2007; Aspalter, 2011; Opielka, 2015; Yang, 2016; Frericks et al., 2018). However, it extends this tradition by specifically developing an ideal type framework focused on basic income principles, creating a novel analytical tool for understanding welfare regimes through a basic income lens. This methodological innovation represents a significant contribution to both welfare regime literature and basic income research.

**Table 1.1** Countries included in the analysis

| *Country* | *Year* |
|---|---|
| Austria | 2009 |
| Belgium | 2013 |
| Finland | 2010 |
| France | 2010 |
| Germany | 2013 |
| Greece | 2014 |
| Italy | 2009 |
| Norway | 2010 |
| Spain | 2010 |
| UK | 2015 |

By applying this ideal type framework to empirical data on job search behaviour across European welfare regimes, the book provides a unique empirical foundation for debates that have often relied more on theoretical assumptions than systematic evidence. The scope thus extends beyond simple country comparisons to identify institutional patterns and causal mechanisms that shape how basic income principles influence labour market behaviour in different contexts.

## Structure of the Book

The book is organised in three parts, each including three chapters. Through this structured approach, the book helps to bridge the gap between theoretical and empirical analysis of basic income, addressing important questions around basic income's potential effects on job search behaviour, and the labour market more broadly.

Part One establishes the theoretical and methodological foundations, defining basic income and its key mechanisms, reviewing the evidence from basic income experiments, and introducing the methodology, qualitative comparative analysis. Chapter two defines basic income and examines how basic income principles manifest as welfare mechanisms which impact on job search behaviour. Chapter three examines the extent of existing knowledge on the potential effects of basic income on job search behaviour, and chapter three introduces the methodological approach taken in researching the potential effects of basic income on job search behaviour across European countries. Chapter four provides an overview of the methodological approach used in this book: qualitative comparative analysis (QCA). It explains the main characteristics of QCA as a methodological approach and how it acts as a bridge between theory and empirical analysis, allowing for a systematic examination of how basic income principles manifest in real world welfare systems, setting up the foundation for later analysis of their effects on job search behaviour.

Part Two, including chapters five, six, and seven, develops and applies the basic income ideal type welfare regime, comparing European welfare regimes to the basic income mechanisms. Chapter five links theory with empirical evidence by developing an ideal type basic income welfare regime based on three key dimensions: unconditionality, universalism, and non-withdrawal of benefits. Chapter six compares ten European welfare regimes and the degrees to which they approximate basic income. Chapter seven develops and applies the methodology for measuring job search intensity, based on time use data, which is then used in part three to examine how different welfare configurations influence behaviours. These chapters bridge theory and practice, grounding the analysis of basic income in institutional realities and establishing a framework for understanding its potential impact on labour market behaviour.

Part Three provides a foundation for more realistic expectations and more effective implementation strategies for basic income. It investigates basic income mechanisms' impact on job search intensity, analysing incentives and disincentives to find work, and exploring the potential impact of basic income through counterfactual analysis to gain a better understanding of basic income's impact across different institutional contexts. Together, chapters eight, nine, and ten demonstrate that basic income's effects are neither linear nor deterministic but emerge from complex interactions between policy mechanisms, institutional contexts, and individual responses. Chapter eight challenges conventional assumptions about work incentives, revealing that supposedly incentivising and disincentivising welfare mechanisms have limited impact on job search behaviour at the aggregate level. Chapter nine examines these empirical findings' implications for basic income policy through counterfactual analysis, exploring how identical basic income schemes might function differently within contrasting welfare contexts, specifically Finland and the UK. Rather than viewing basic income as inherently incentivising work, this analysis reconceptualizes it as enhancing income security within specific institutional frameworks. Finally, Chapter ten synthesises the book's insights, highlighting key lessons for research and policy development. It emphasises how institutional contexts mediate welfare effects, challenges assumptions about work incentives, and outlines promising directions for future inquiry and policy implementation. Overall, Part Three provides a foundation for more realistic expectations and more effective implementation strategies, and how this study moves the academic debate forward.

## References

Aspalter, C. (2011). The development of ideal-typical welfare regime theory. *International Social Work, 54*(6), 735–750. https://doi.org/10.1177/0020872810393765

Bambra, C. (2007). Defamilisation and welfare state regimes: A cluster analysis. *International Journal of Social Welfare, 16*(4), 326–338. https://doi.org/10.1111/j.1468-2397.2007.00486.x

Benhabib, J., & Bull, C. (1983). Job search: The choice of intensity. *Journal of Political Economy, 91*(5), 747–764. https://doi.org/10.1086/261180

Bloemen, H. G. (2005). Job search, search intensity, and labor market transitions: An empirical analysis. *Journal of Human Resources, 40*(1), 232–269.

Duşa, A. (2020). Set theoretic methods. In *The SAGE handbook of research methods in political science and international relations* (pp. 1097–1116). SAGE Publications Ltd. Retrieved April 21, 2025, from https://www.torrossa.com/gs/resourceProxy?an=5018785&publisher=FZ7200#page=1142

Esping-Andersen, G. (1990). *The three worlds of welfare capitalism*. Princeton University Press. Retrieved March 27, 2024, from https://books.google.com/books?hl=en&lr=&id=ERCnDwAAQBAJ&oi=fnd&pg=PR8&dq=three+worlds+of+welfare+capitalism&ots=0EcmiFe_Uv&sig=2lh58kMmmKErWBF7jdUVGplpIjY

Esping-Andersen, G. (1999). *Social foundations of postindustrial economies*. Oxford University Press. Retrieved April 21, 2024, from https://books.google.com/books?hl=en&lr=&id=yeXnCwAAQBAJ&oi=fnd&pg=PR7&dq=Esping%E2%80%90Andersen,+G.+(1999)+Social+Foundations+of+Postindustrial+Economies,+Oxford:+Oxford+University+Press.+&ots=rt8GjBBsFi&sig=lO4_tIaI8L9IM-O62PzeW4ZxahI

Faberman, J., & Kudlyak, M. (2014). The intensity of job search and search duration. Retrieved April 21, 2025, from https://papers.ssrn.com/sol3/papers.cfm?abstract_id=2442910

Faberman, R. J., & Kudlyak, M. (2019). The intensity of job search and search duration. *American Economic Journal: Macroeconomics, 11*(3), 327–357.

Ferrera, M. (1996). The 'Southern Model' of Welfare in Social Europe. *Journal of European Social Policy, 6*(1), 17–37. https://doi.org/10.1177/095892879600600102

Frericks, P., Höppner, J., & Och, R. (2018). The Difficulty of Measuring Institutions: A Methodological Approach to the Comparative Analysis of Institutions. *Social Indicators Research, 137*(3), 847–865. https://doi.org/10.1007/s11205-017-1638-9

Krueger, A. B., & Mueller, A. I. (2012). The lot of the unemployed: A time use perspective. *Journal of the European Economic Association, 10*(4), 765–794.

Leibfried, S. (2002). Towards a European welfare state? In *New perspectives on the welfare state in Europe* (pp. 128–151). Routledge. Retrieved April 21, 2024, from https://www.taylorfrancis.com/chapters/edit/10.4324/9780203415863-17/towards-european-welfare-state-stephan-leibfried

Minogue, R. (2018). Five problems with basic income. *Third Way*. https://www.thirdway.org/memo/five-problems-with-universal-basic-income

Opielka, M. (2015). The feasibility of a basic income: Implications for social policy and social work. In: *Social policy and social dimensions of vulnerability and resilience in Europe* (pp. 35–46).

Raventós, D. (2007). Basic income. *The Material Conditions of Freedom*, London.

Swaine, L. (2011). Work lovers, freedom, and basic income. *Contemporary Political Theory, 10*(1). https://philpapers.org/rec/SWAWLF

Titmuss, R. M. (1974). Social Policy. Allen & Unwin.

Van Parijs, P. (1992). Arguing for Basic income. *Ethical Foundations for a Radical reform*. https://dial.uclouvain.be/pr/boreal/object/boreal:96711

Van Parijs, P. (2017). Why surfers should be fed: The liberal case for an unconditional basic income. *In Distributive Justice* (pp. 483–513). Routledge.

White, J. (2023). Universal Basic Income: A pointless trial of a bad idea, Institute of Economic Affairs. https://iea.org.uk/universal-basic-income-a-pointless-trial-of-a-bad-idea/

Widerquist, K., & Lewis, M. A. (2006). An efficiency argument for the basic income guarantee. *International Journal of Environment, Workplace and Employment, 2*(1), 21. https://doi.org/10.1504/IJEWE.2006.009356

Wilensky, H. L. (1974). *The welfare state and equality: Structural and ideological roots of public expenditures*. Univ of California Press. Retrieved April 21, 2024, from https://books.google.com/books?hl=en&lr=&id=5zaa84FFNLwC&oi=fnd&pg=PR11&dq=Wilensky,+H.+L.+(1975).+The+Welfare+State+and+Equality:+Structural+and+Ideological++Roots+of+Public+Expenditures.+London:+University+of+California+Press&ots=0aCMOV3DJT&sig=GsqK0Os8R9Bsxj8dx6NEamuGJ00

Yang, N. (2016). *Explaining welfare development in East Asia by using set-theoretic methods: East Asia in transition*. PhD Thesis. University of York. Retrieved April 21, 2024, from https://etheses.whiterose.ac.uk/15607/

# Part I

CHAPTER 2

# Basic Income Principles, Welfare Mechanisms, and Labour Market Responses

**Abstract** This chapter defines basic income and examines the dimensions that underpin it. It focuses on three principles that are fundamental to a basic income, and which relate to the potential impact of a basic income on job search behaviour amongst unemployed people. The three principles are unconditionality, universalism and non-withdrawal of benefits. From these core principles, three welfare mechanisms are identified, which link basic income to existing welfare regimes. It is from this link between theoretical principles and welfare mechanisms that the analysis throughout this book is developed. The importance of this chapter and of the book more broadly is in linking abstract theoretical terms, such as universalism, to empirically grounded welfare mechanisms that shape existing welfare regimes and their impacts on behaviour. By developing these links, we gain a better understanding of how basic income would function, its potential impact on job search behaviour and labour market participation more broadly.

**Keywords** Unconditionality and conditionality · Universalism and selectivism · Non-withdrawal of benefits · Unemployment trap · Participation tax rates · Work incentives · Welfare mechanisms



S. Watkins, *Basic Income, Work Incentives and Job Search Behaviour*, Exploring the Basic Income Guarantee,
https://doi.org/10.1007/978-3-031-99197-4_2

## Defining Basic Income and Translating into Practice

At its most simple, Basic income is a means of transferring money to people. The main principles that define basic income are as follows.

- Universal. It is paid to everyone within a defined political community (i.e. state, country). As such, it is non-contributory and eligibility is not dependent on any previous social insurance contributions or identified category of need.
- Unconditional. Payment is not dependent on the demonstration of certain types of behaviours (i.e. undertaking or looking for paid work).
- Individual. It is paid to each individual as a right. It is not based on household composition, so each household member receives their basic income separately.
- Not means-tested. It is not withdrawn as income from other sources increases.
- Non-withdrawable. It is not withdrawn when a person's circumstances change, e.g. when moving from unemployment into work.
- Paid regularly. It is not a lump sum, but is paid in regular instalments, generally conceived as weekly or monthly payments.
- Paid at a single, flat rate to everyone.[1]
- Permanent (or as permanent as any welfare programme can be). This means that it is paid throughout life, and a dependable source of income.

It is important to note that the definition of basic income deliberately excludes certain important characteristics of any welfare regime, notably, the amount to be paid and the funding mechanisms. This highlights the distinction between basic income and a basic income *scheme*. Whilst the above definition sets out what a basic income looks like in theory, a basic income scheme sets out how a basic income is implemented in practice. This includes the amount to be paid, the method(s) of funding and any changes made to existing tax and benefits. Whilst there is only one basic income, there may be any number of different basic

[1] TThere are suggestions for basic income schemes which pay a lower amount 'to' children and a different, usually higher amount to pensioners ( e.g. Torry, 2022).

income schemes, with varying levels of payment, different funding mechanisms and accompanied by a range of taxes alongside a variety of other welfare schemes. A basic income scheme therefore places basic income within a specific context. For example, the principle of universalism is central to basic income (Andersson & Kangas, 2007; Danson et al., 2012; Mays & Tomlinson, 2019). It simply means it is paid to everyone within a defined political community. However, from a practical perspective, the term 'everyone' needs further definition. In practice, basic income universality is inherently constrained by political reality. This would most likely be in the form of a test of residence. For example, people defined as legally resident in the UK would be eligible to receive basic income. People who cease to be resident, or are in the UK, perhaps on a working visa, are not eligible to receive basic income. This is the link between theoretical principle and empirical reality that this book provides.

Although it is often assumed that basic income is paid by the state and funded through taxation, this is not explicitly defined, and there are various ways in which a basic income could be funded aside from through taxation, for example through the 'sovereign money' (Crocker, 2020). When not funded by taxation, it is more commonly framed as a 'social dividend' payment, separate from existing welfare systems (Standing, 2019). However, this book views basic income as a welfare policy, which may either replace or augment certain existing benefits, for example social assistance. From this perspective, basic income is framed as a welfare type payment funded through the taxation system. Whilst basic income is deemed to be a 'radical' departure from existing welfare schemes, many existing welfare regimes incorporate some of the characteristics of basic income. Three examples of different welfare benefits highlight this point: unemployment insurance, state pensions and social assistance.

Unemployment insurance shares certain characteristics with basic income. It is commonly paid on an individual basis, irrespective of household income or living arrangements, and is not means-tested. However, it is invariably accompanied by behavioural conditions related to job search activities. It is also time-limited, so expires after a certain period. It is paid only to the unemployed and eligibility is contingent on an individual's previous work record and social insurance contributions, so not universal. It is also withdrawn when the recipient moves into paid work. It therefore fulfils the individual requirement, and the non means-tested requirement, but fails the remaining requirements of basic income.

Similar to basic income, state provided pensions are not means-tested, nor do they have any behavioural conditions attached. They are also largely individual benefits. They are non-withdrawable in that, once benefits start, they do not stop until the individual dies. However, pension schemes only pay out once a certain age is reached and eligibility is largely dependent on a record of national insurance contributions from paid work. Given the age restrictions and eligibility requirements, they cannot be classed as universal. State pensions are closer to basic income in principle than unemployment benefits. They are not means-tested, unconditional, largely individual and non-withdrawable. However, they fail the universal requirements as eligibility is limited to those above pension age and is defined by previous social security contributions.

Social assistance schemes are non-contributory, commonly flat rate cash benefits paid for an unlimited time, or as long as there is a demonstrable financial need. To some degree, they are therefore universal. However, they are means-tested, with other sources of income taken into account when determining eligibility and entitlement. Means-testing commonly includes the income and assets of others in the same household, so they cannot truly be classed as individual. They also increasingly come with behavioural conditions attached, related to finding work if unemployed, or increasing the number of hours worked if already in employment. Social assistance therefore fulfils the non-contributory and the flat rate requirements but falls short of the remaining requirements for basic income. Although, it has commonly been thought that social assistance would be the easiest existing policy to convert into a basic income, given its characteristics as a flat rate, non-contributory payment, as this comparison shows, significant administrative changes would still be required to transform social assistance schemes into a basic income.

The examples above highlight the similarities, as well as the significant differences, between existing benefits and basic income. They also demonstrate that in the worlds of welfare, there are rarely, if ever, examples of benefits that are truly universal, unconditional or individual. Instead, each welfare regime contains degrees of universality, unconditionality and individualism. This is why it is important to examine basic income within the context of existing welfare regimes. It helps us think about the mechanisms that currently exist across welfare states, how they impact on behaviour, and how basic income may change these causal mechanisms.

## A New Analytical Approach: Ideal Type Analysis

This book develops an analytical framework that examines how welfare systems embody basic income principles to varying degrees. These create natural variations that we can study to understand their effects on job search behaviour. Each defining principle of basic income exists to some degree across welfare regimes. As such, this book uses basic income principles to measure the degrees to which existing welfare regimes approximate basic income by translating basic income principles into measurable welfare mechanisms.

It does this by firstly understanding that each principle has an antithesis or antitheses in welfare literature, and that each exists on a spectrum rather than as a binary condition of being present or absent across different welfare regimes. The methodological approach uses these spectrums to measure basic income principles in existing welfare regimes. It allows researchers to move beyond binary comparisons, measuring more nuanced differences in policy design and their impacts on behaviour.

The focus of this book is on the job search activities of unemployed people, so examines the principles of basic income identified as most pertinent to job search behaviour:

- Unconditional
- Universal
- Non-withdrawable

### *Unconditional—Conditional*

The antithesis of unconditional is conditional. Basic income requires the complete absence of conditionality, whereas existing welfare systems display varying levels of conditionality. The main issue is thus determining degrees of (un)conditionality.

Conditionality refers to the behavioural requirements for ongoing receipt of benefits, and the administrative processes that accompany them. It has become an increasingly important characteristic of welfare states internationally; designed to increase labour market participation amongst both unemployed people, and increasingly those already in work. Conditionality operates through three distinct mechanisms (Watts & Fitzpatrick, 2018).

1. Behavioural Requirements

Behavioural requirements define the actions individuals must undertake to maintain eligibility and entitlement to benefits. These requirements commonly define the scope of job search activity, the jobs that the unemployed individual should apply for, and those which they may legitimately refuse without facing sanctions. They may also stipulate the quantity of job search activity, i.e. how much time they are expected to spend in job search activities, and/or the minimum number of applications to be submitted.

2. Monitoring

The second mechanism is the monitoring function used by those administrating benefits to ensure compliance with behavioural requirements and related administrative tasks. Monitoring is designed to ensure that the required job search activities are undertaken.

3. Sanctions

The third mechanism is the punitive element of conditionality, taking the form of sanctions. Sanctions are commonly in the form of financial penalties, specifically the withdrawal of benefits for a specified period of time or permanently. The threat and application of sanctions represent the enforcement mechanism that give behavioural requirements their coercive power.

The empirical evidence regarding the effects of conditionality on job search behaviour and labour market outcomes more broadly demonstrates a complex picture, distinguishable between short term and longer term outcomes. Empirical evidence consistently shows that conditionality can reduce the length of time spent on unemployment benefits and increases rates of short term employment. Several studies have linked increased levels of monitoring, through more frequent contact with employment services and monitoring of job search activities, with reduced periods spent on unemployment benefits (Dolton & O'Neill, 2002; Gorter & Kalb, 1996; Johnson & Klepinger, 1994; McVicar, 2008; Setty, 2019). Studies have also focused on the effect of sanctions. However, the results appear to vary depending on geographical location. Research across several European countries, including the Netherlands (Abbring et al., 2005), Switzerland (Lalive et al., 2005) and Germany (Boockmann et al., 2014) found that individuals facing sanctions showed a higher propensity to work. However, comparable research in the United States, found no such effects (Wu et al., 2014) and a comprehensive analysis of welfare conditionality across 21 countries ranging between 1980 and 2012 found that whilst higher job search activity requirements led to increased employment, tougher sanctions demonstrated no similar short term effects (Knotz, 2020). Conversely, there are unintended consequences in long term outcomes.

The overall picture is that conditionality reduces unemployment in the short term. However, evidence also suggests that higher levels of conditionality may be counterproductive in the longer term, resulting in increased levels of future unemployment spells, where quick returns to ill-suited employment often lead to repeated unemployment (Arni et al., 2013; Fording et al., 2013). This has knocked on effects on wages, job quality and employment stability as conditionality pushes people into precarious, low paid, and less suitable jobs, which do not align with their needs and preferences, helping to explain repeated spells of unemployment (Watts et al., 2014). Whilst sanctions were found to successfully remove people from claiming benefits in the UK, many of them remained jobless (National Audit Office, 2016). This suggests that for a significant number of benefit recipients, monitoring can push them out of the benefits' system completely, without finding work, an unintended consequence, which increases the risk of poverty amongst this group (Loopstra et al., 2015). However, what would the effects of reduced conditionality be?

The effects of conditionality on specific demographic groups can be particularly problematic. Research focusing on lone parents in the UK found that raising work-related criteria resulted in short term employment, but this was frequently followed by a swift return to the welfare system (Finn & Gloster, 2010). This cycle of employment and unemployment increase the risk of poverty as people may lose benefits which they cannot financially replace. Interestingly, evidence suggests that either reducing or removing conditionality may have positive labour market outcomes. There is evidence that the removal of monitoring requirements is associated with increased participation in training and education

(McVicar, 2008). This suggests that when people are freed from immediate work requirements, many will invest in improving their longer term employability.

There is also evidence that allowing unemployed people more time to find a suitable job can result in lower secondary periods of unemployment (Johnson & Klepinger, 1994). This challenges the argument that the primary role of welfare regimes should be immediate re-employment.

Overall, the evidence suggests that whilst conditionality can be effective in moving people from unemployment benefits into employment, it may be counterproductive for long term unemployment outcomes and overall wellbeing. Conversely, there is evidence that the removal of conditionality, specifically monitoring results in more people pursuing non-work activities, particularly education and training, and that people taking longer to find work may lead to improved job matches, resulting in fewer subsequent periods of unemployment. This supports the argument made by basic income advocates (e.g. Standing, 2011) that the removal of behavioural conditionality would enable people to make longer term choices about their future that would otherwise not be feasible given the requirement to find paid work to maintain benefits.

### *Universal—Selective or Targeted*

In basic income literature, the term 'universalism' relates to the fact that it is paid to everyone within a specified political community. It denotes the absence of circumstantial requirements for eligibility beyond citizenship or residence in a community (Van Parijs & Vanderborght, 2017). Receipt of basic income is not dependent on the occurrence of a specific social risk, nor on membership of a particular sub-population group, such as the unemployed, nor on previous social insurance contributions.

Welfare universalism is a complex concept with multiple meanings across different contexts (Stefánsson, 2012). Whilst various forms of universalism exist (Anttonen & Sipilä, 2014), the core concept emphasises inclusion, sameness, and unity (Stefánsson, 2012). It primarily focuses on coverage and equality in welfare provision (Bergh, 2004). These principles align closely with the philosophical foundation of basic income.

The antitheses of universalism can be characterised by two methods of differentiating between groups who are eligible for benefits. The first is the categorisation of benefits based on the characteristics of individuals or household members, where sets of programmes are designed for different identifiable groups, such as people who are unemployed or retired (Esping-Andersen, 1990). This form of differentiation has been described as Selectivism (Hultqvist & Hollertz, 2021; Kim, 2021; Kuivalainen & Niemelä, 2010). The second method is the targeting of benefits based on financial resources, where eligibility is based on a demonstrable financial need. Financial targeting of benefits uses means-testing as a mechanism to identify those who are eligible, meaning that benefits are reserved to those on low incomes and low levels of wealth (Anttonen et al., 2012).

In theory, the provision of universal benefits may act as a disincentive to look for work, particularly where the payments cover basic needs. This would be particularly evident at the aggregate level, as everyone would receive payments, which are under existing welfare regimes, limited to specific groups of recipients. However, there is no literature specifically linking the relationship between 'universalism' and labour market participation or job search intensity amongst the unemployed. Analysis of unemployment insurance is usually framed through the generosity of unemployment insurance, as well as its duration. This book addresses this gap in the literature, explicitly measuring the degree of universalism of an unemployment scheme, through the concept of accessibility and examining its impact on job search intensity.

### *Non-Withdrawable—Withdrawable*

Basic income is defined as non-withdrawable, so it is neither withdrawn when a person's status changes, for example when they move from being unemployed to employed, neither is it means-tested away as income from other sources increases.

In this book, the term benefit withdrawal relates are two interrelated mechanisms that help to shape how welfare systems impact on behaviour. The first mechanism is the removal of categorical benefits when moving from unemployment into employment. This is usually in the form of a loss of entitlement to unemployment benefits on taking up employment. The second mechanism is the reduction of means-tested benefits as income from other sources increases. As existing welfare regimes commonly combine both kinds of benefits, those moving from unemployment into employment are often faced being little or no better off financially being in work, compared to being unemployed. The combined effects of these can often result in very high marginal tax rates on additional earnings.

This combined mechanism creates significant financial disincentives to enter into employment due to the high marginal rates on additional earned income. The rational economic choice in such circumstances would be to remain unemployed or not increase working hours. This situation has been described as the 'unemployment trap'.

The unemployment trap results from the complex interaction of benefits, tax and social insurance systems and income from employment. It is formally defined as the ratio between the change in disposable income for individuals who are not currently employed who then enter the workforce (Torry, 2017).

A worked example helps to highlight the impact of the unemployment trap.

Marc is a 35-year old, living on his own in Belgium.[2] He has been unemployed for 2 months and claims unemployment benefits. His previous salary was €31,122, equivalent to two-thirds of the average wage in Belgium.

Marc gets a full-time job on the same salary he was on at the time of becoming unemployed. Although his gross income increases by €11,884, his net income only increases by €758, due to the removal of benefits and the income tax and social insurance contributions payable on his salary (Table 2.1). The effective rate of tax on his new earnings is 94%.[3] This example demonstrates the high participation tax rates which result in the 'unemployment trap'.

**Table 2.1** Gross and net income in unemployment

| *Income and deductions* | *Unemployed* | *Employed* |
|---|---|---|
| Gross salary | – | € 31,122 |
| Unemployment benefits | € 19,238 | – |
| Income tax | – | – € 6,795 |
| Social insurance | – | – € 4,332 |
| Net income | € 19,238 | € 19,996 |

[2] The example is based on 2014 figures, which is the year analysed for Belgium and assumes that Marc has 14 years of social insurance contributions.

[3] The figures were based on the TAXBEN model provided by the OECD, which can be accessed here: OECD calculator of taxes and benefits | OECD.

In contrast to existing benefits, basic income is neither withdrawable nor means-tested, so payments under a basic income continue regardless of changes in employment status or level of earnings. Whilst basic income may be taxable (depending on the nature of the basic income scheme), the mechanism differs fundamentally from traditional welfare benefits. Under basic income, individuals may face a point in the income scale where they become net contributors rather than net beneficiaries, but they do not encounter the cliff edges characterised by withdrawable and means-tested benefits when entering employment.

Despite the obvious financial disincentive to find paid work caused by high participation tax rates, the claim that high participation tax rates have a negative effect on transitions from unemployment to employment is not supported by empirical evidence. The basic income experiment, conducted in Finland between 2017 and 2019, specifically addressed this issue. During the experiment, participation tax rates for recipients of the basic income were deliberately designed to be far lower than those in the control group. Overall, the experiment lowered participation tax rates by an average of 23 percentage points for those in the treatment group, compared to the control group. Despite the significant reductions in disincentives to work, there were no significant changes in employment amongst the unemployed (Verho et al., 2022).

These findings cast doubt on the prevailing assumption that financial disincentives are a determinant factor in job search behaviour. Whilst the unemployment trap represents a real financial barrier to entering employment for many people, its actual impact on individuals' decision making appears more limited than theoretical expectations would predict.

## Basic Income Principles and Conflicting Work Incentives

The basic income principles identified in this chapter, when combined, may produce conflicting incentives and disincentives to find paid work as Fig. 2.1 demonstrates. According to theoretical expectations, the lack of conditionality may act as a disincentive to find work, as there is no requirement to look for work for ongoing entitlement to basic income. In contrast, the non-withdrawal of basic income means that there is a financial incentive to find work, as people will get to keep more of their income from paid work, than under existing welfare regimes with high participation tax rates. Finally, the provision of universal payments may disincentivise job search as everyone would receive them, rather than only those who qualify by reason of being, for example, unemployed. The interaction of these three mechanisms will therefore guide the effects of basic income, as they guide the effects of existing welfare regimes.

This diagram illustrates the complex relationships between the three defining mechanisms of basic income and their potential effects on job search behaviour. The three outer circles represent the key mechanisms:

1. **Unconditionality**: The absence of behavioural requirements, monitoring and the threat of sanctions may reduce immediate pressure to search for work, potentially decreasing search intensity in the short term.
2. **Non-withdrawal**: The retention of benefits upon entering employment ensures that work always pays, potentially increasing motivation to search for suitable jobs.

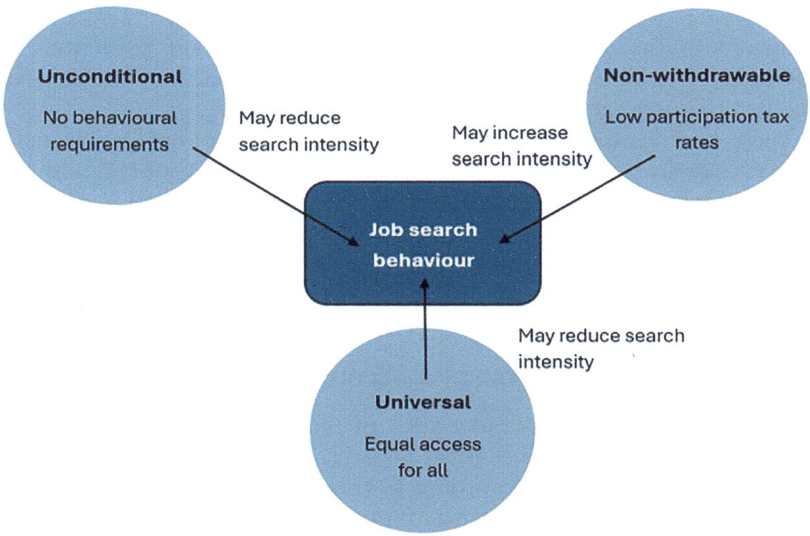


**Fig. 2.1** Interactions between basic income mechanisms and job search behaviour

3. **Universalism:** Equal access for all members of society may reduce job search incentives, particularly for those who were not previously eligible for benefits.

This visual framework helps explain why examining these mechanisms in isolation may provide incomplete or misleading conclusions about basic income's potential effects on labour market participation. It also highlights the importance of considering institutional and social context when analysing how these mechanisms might interact in practice.

The analytical framework developed in this book works particularly well in analysing how institutional contexts mediate policy effects. By examining how different combinations of basic income principles affect job search behaviour across various welfare regimes, we gain a better understanding of how basic income might function in different institutional, social and cultural settings. This addresses a key limitation of both experimental studies, which often ignore institutional context, and purely theoretical approaches, which may oversimplify behavioural responses.

## Bridging Theory and Practice: Basic Income Mechanisms in Context

This chapter defined basic income, examined its underlying principles and identified their antitheses to enable comparisons to be made between basic income and existing welfare regimes. It identified and examined three welfare mechanisms based on to their potential effects on job search intensity; conditionality, universalism and non-withdrawal, drawing out similarities and differences between basic income and welfare regimes in practice, before examining the empirical evidence linking each mechanism to job search behaviour and labour market participation more broadly. The evidence suggests complex and sometimes contradictory relationships between these mechanisms and job search behaviour. Removing conditionality may reduce immediate job search intensity but enable better long term employment outcomes. Non-withdrawal of benefits provides clear financial incentives for employment, though evidence suggests such incentives may be less important than assumed. The effects of universalism on job search behaviour remain less studied but may reduce incentives to search for paid work, by dint of being paid to everyone.

The analytical framework used in this book recognises that welfare regimes already contain varying degrees of basic income principles. By studying how different combinations of these principles affect behaviour across existing welfare regimes, we can better predict how basic income might function in different institutional contexts.

This approach addresses key limitations in existing basic income research. Whilst experiments provide valuable insights, their temporary nature and specific contexts limit their generalisability, whereas theoretical approaches may oversimplify behavioural responses. By examining how basic income principles manifest in existing welfare systems, we can study their long term effects across different institutional settings.

The next chapter examines empirical evidence from various basic income and related experiments conducted across developed welfare states. It evaluates how closely each experiment approximates the key principles of basic income introduced in this chapter and analyses their empirical findings on labour market effects. It builds a framework for assessing these experiments, then explores three categories of evidence: natural experiments like the Alaskan Permanent Dividend, recent basic income trials in Europe and North America, and historic Negative Income Tax experiments. Through this analysis, the chapter identifies consistent patterns in how basic income affects work behaviour whilst highlighting the limitations of experimental evidence and proposing priorities for future research.

## References

Abbring, J. H., Van den Berg, G. J., & Van Ours, J. C. (2005). The effect of unemployment insurance sanctions on the transition rate from unemployment to employment. *The Economic Journal, 115*(505), 602–630.

Andersson, J.O., & Kangas, O.E. (2007). Universalism in the age of workfare: attitudes to basic income in Sweden and Finland. In *Normative foundations of the welfare state* (pp. 124–141). Routledge. Retrieved April 21, 2025, from https://www.taylorfrancis.com/chapters/edit/10.4324/9780203695241-17/universalism-age-workfare-attitudes-basic-income-sweden-finland-jan-otto-andersson-olli-kangas

Anttonen, A., et al. (2012). Universalism and the challenge of diversity. In *Welfare state, universalism and diversity*. Edward Elgar Publishing. Retrieved April 20, 2024, from https://www.elgaronline.com/downloadpdf/edcollchap/9781849803830.00006.pdf

Anttonen, A., & Sipilä, J. (2014). *Varieties of universalism.* Draft Paper Prepared for the UNRISD Conference, New Directions in Social Policy: Alternatives from and for the Global South, 7–8.

Arni, P., Lalive, R., & Van Ours, J. C. (2013). How effective are unemployment benefit sanctions? Looking beyond unemployment exit. *Journal of Applied Econometrics, 28*(7), 1153–1178. https://doi.org/10.1002/jae.2289

Bergh, A. (2004). The Universal Welfare State: Theory and the Case of Sweden. *Political Studies, 52*(4), 745–766. https://doi.org/10.1111/j.1467-9248.2004.00506.x

Boockmann, B. L., Thomsen, S., & Walter, T. (2014). Intensifying the use of benefit sanctions: An effective tool to increase employment? *IZA Journal of Labor Policy, 3*(1), 21. https://doi.org/10.1186/2193-9004-3-21

Crocker, G. (2020). *Basic income and sovereign money: The alternative to economic crisis and austerity policy.* Springer Nature.

Danson, M., et al. (2012). The case for universalism. *An assessment of the evidence on the effectiveness* [Preprint]. Retrieved April 21, 2025, from https://reidfoundation.scot/wp-content/uploads/2012/12/The-Case-for-Universalism2.pdf

Dolton, P., & O'Neill, D. (2002). The long-run effects of unemployment monitoring and work-search programs: Experimental evidence from the United Kingdom. *Journal of Labor Economics, 20*(2), 381–403. https://doi.org/10.1086/338686

Esping-Andersen, G. (1990) *The three worlds of welfare capitalism.* Princeton University Press. Retrieved March 27, 2024, from https://books.google.com/books?hl=en&lr=&id=ERCnDwAAQBAJ&oi=fnd&pg=PR8&dq=three+worlds+of+welfare+capitalism&ots=0EcmiFe_Uv&sig=2lh58kMmmKErWBF7jdUVGplpIjY

Finn, D., & Gloster, R. (2010) *Lone parent obligations: A review of recent evidence on the work-related requirements within the benefit systems of different countries.* Department for Work and Pensions. Retrieved April 20, 2024, from https://researchportal.port.ac.uk/en/publications/lone-parent-obligations-a-review-of-recent-evidence-on-the-work-r

Fording, R. C., Schram, S. F., & Soss, J. (2013). Do welfare sanctions help or hurt the poor? Estimating the causal effect of sanctioning on client earnings. *Social Service Review, 87*(4), 641–676. https://doi.org/10.1086/674111

Gorter, C., & Kalb, G. R. (1996). Estimating the effect of counseling and monitoring the unemployed using a job search model. *Journal of Human Resources, 31*, 590–610.

Hultqvist, S., & Hollertz, K. (2021). Individual need and societal claims: Challenging the understanding of universalism versus selectivism in social policy. *Social Policy & Administration, 55*(5), 940–953. https://doi.org/10.1111/spol.12680

Johnson, T. R., & Klepinger, D. H. (1994). Experimental evidence on unemployment insurance work-search policies. *Journal of Human Resources, 29*, 695–717.

Kim, S.-Y. (2021). An exploratory study upon the determinants of welfare attitudes on universalism vs. selectivism. *The Journal of the Convergence on Culture Technology, 7*(2), 191–197.

Knotz, C. M. (2020). Does demanding activation work? A comparative analysis of the effects of unemployment benefit conditionality on employment in 21 advanced economies, 1980–2012. *European Sociological Review, 36*(1), 121–135.

Kuivalainen, S., & Niemelä, M. (2010). From universalism to selectivism: The ideational turn of the anti-poverty policies in Finland. *Journal of European Social Policy, 20*(3), 263–276. https://doi.org/10.1177/0958928710364432

Lalive, R., Van Ours, J. C., & Zweimüller, J. (2005). The effect of benefit sanctions on the duration of unemployment. *Journal of the European Economic Association, 3*(6), 1386–1417.

Loopstra, R., Reeves, A., Taylor-Robinson, D., Barr, B., McKee, M. & Stuckler, D. (2015). Austerity, sanctions, and the rise of food banks in the UK. *Bmj, 350.*

Mays, J., & Tomlinson, J. (2019). Basic income and a new universalism. *Social Alternatives, 38*(2), 3–10.

McVicar, D. (2008). Job search monitoring intensity, unemployment exit and job entry: Quasi-experimental evidence from the UK. *Labour Economics, 15*(6), 1451–1468.

National Audit Office. (2016). Local Welfare Provision. National Audit Office.

Setty, O. (2019). Optimal unemployment insurance with monitoring. *Quantitative Economics, 10*(2), 693–733. https://doi.org/10.3982/QE564

Standing, G. (2011). The precariat: The new dangerous class (p. 208). Bloomsbury academic.

Standing, G. (2019). Basic income as common dividends: Piloting a transformative policy. In *Progressive economy forum.* Retrieved April 1, 2025, from https://mronline.org/wp-content/uploads/2019/09/PEF_Piloting_Basic_Income_Guy_Standing.pdf

Stefánsson, K. (2012). What is in a word? Universalism, ideology and practice. *Welfare State, Universalism and Diversity*, 42–68.

Torry, M. (2017). *A variety of indicators evaluated for two implementation methods for a Citizen's Basic Income*. EUROMOD Working Paper. Retrieved March 29, 2024, from https://www.econstor.eu/handle/10419/197610

Torry, M. (2022). *Two feasible Basic Income schemes for the UK, and a feasible pilot project for Scotland* (No. CeMPA WP 7/22). CeMPA Working Paper Series.

Van Parijs, P., & Vanderborght, Y. (2017). Basic income: A radical proposal for a free society and a sane economy. *Harvard University Press*. https://doi.org/10.4159/9780674978072

Verho, J., Hämäläinen, K., & Kanninen, O. (2022). Removing welfare traps: Employment responses in the Finnish basic income experiment. *American Economic Journal: Economic Policy, 14*(1), 501–522. https://doi.org/10.1257/pol.20200143

Watts, B., & Fitzpatrick, S. (2018). *Welfare conditionality*. Routledge. Retrieved April 22, 2025, from https://www.taylorfrancis.com/books/mono/10.4324/9781315652047/welfare-conditionality-beth-watts-suzanne-fitzpatrick

Watts, B., Fitzpatrick, S., Bramley, G. & Watkins, D. (2014). Welfare Sanctions and Conditionality in the UK. Joseph Rowntree Foundation.

Wu, C.-F., Cancian, M., & Wallace, G. (2014). The effect of welfare sanctions on TANF exits and employment. *Children and Youth Services Review, 36*, 1–14.

CHAPTER 3

# Empirical Evidence from Basic Income Experiments

**Abstract** This chapter explores empirical evidence from a variety of basic income and related experiments. It measures the degree to which they approximate the principles of basic income to assess the degree to which they may be classed as basic income experiments. Each section examines empirical findings in relation to labour market effects, and where possible job search behaviours across experiments. Lessons for basic income policy are drawn whilst acknowledging the constraints of experimental evidence. The approach taken lays the groundwork for the empirical analysis of existing welfare systems that follows in subsequent chapters.

**Keywords** Basic income experiments · Negative income tax experiments · Labour market effects · Experimental limitations · Employment outcomes

An ever growing number of experiments labelled as 'basic income', provide an increasing amount of data on various impacts of the interventions across a range of contexts and populations. Whilst these are an important source of information about the potential effects of basic income on labour market behaviour, care must be taken when interpreting and generalising their findings. It is important to recognise the degrees to



S. Watkins, *Basic Income, Work Incentives and Job Search Behaviour*, Exploring the Basic Income Guarantee,
https://doi.org/10.1007/978-3-031-99197-4_3

which each experiment actually reflects the key principles of basic income identified in chapter one and whether what is being tested can indeed be classed as basic income or an approximation of it. Many experiments lack key principles of basic income through a combination of political, financial, and legal constraints (Neuwinger, 2022), which restrict our capacity to evaluate their effects.

The chapter examines major experiments in three categories:

1. Natural experiments. Policies and experiments which are not designed as basic income experiments but nevertheless share many of its characteristics
2. Recent basic income experiments in Europe and North America. This covers the 'second wave' of basic income experiments which began in the mid-2010s.
3. Historic negative income tax experiments in North America. This section covers the experiments in the late 1960s and the 1970s.

To introduce the analytical framework used to evaluate basic income experiments, the diagram outlines key elements including the extent to which core basic income principles are present or absent, specific design features of each experiment, and the broader institutional and social context in which they were implemented. It also identifies the range of observed labour market behaviours and maps the methodological approaches used in each case, along with their respective limitations. This structured lens provides a comprehensive basis for comparing experiments and assessing their relevance to real-world policy applications (Fig. 3.1).

## Limitations of Basic Income Experiments

Before discussing the lessons that can be drawn from the empirical evidence discussed in this section, it is important to highlight the limitations of experiments that reduce our ability to generalise about the findings. Although each experiment has its own specific limitations and methodological issues, there are limitations applicable to all, which impact on our ability to draw firm conclusions. These limitations are discussed below.

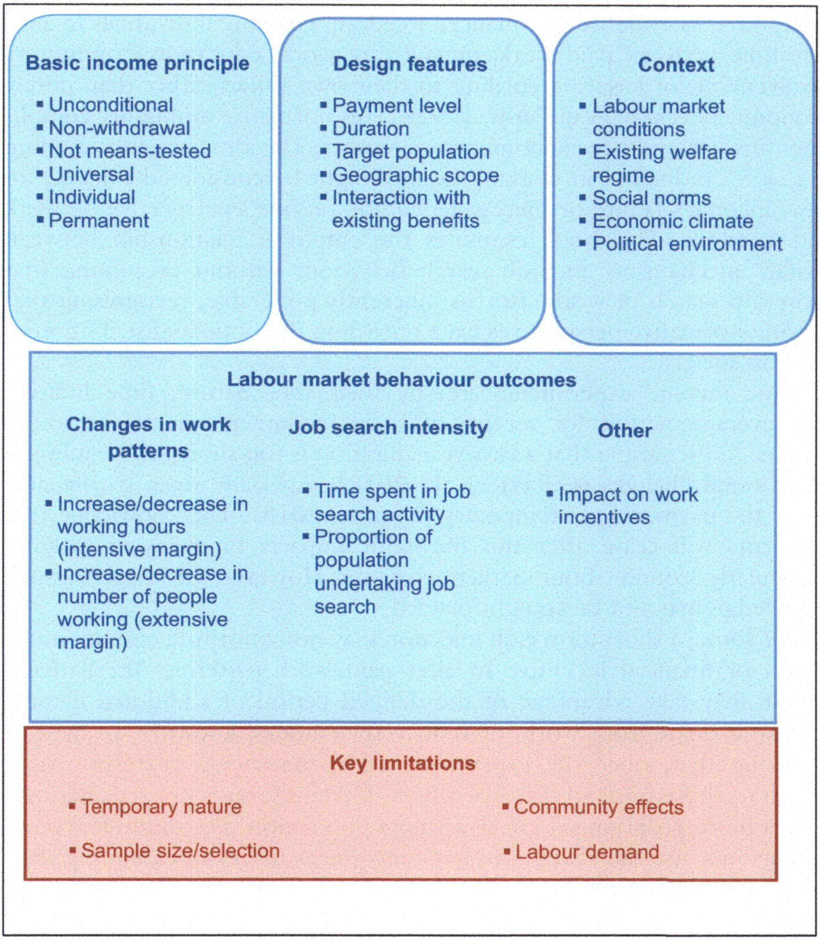


**Fig. 3.1** Evaluation framework for basic income experiments

When interpreting experimental results, an important consideration is the normative framework through which labour market effects are evaluated. Experimental findings of modest reductions in work hours or labour force participation are frequently interpreted as evidence of problematic work disincentives. However, the same empirical findings can be interpreted as evidence of enhanced freedom, enabling individuals to allocate time between paid work, unpaid care work, education, community involvement, or leisure according to their own values rather than purely economic necessity (Van Parijs, 1992). This normative ambiguity complicates how we evaluate experimental outcomes. The same empirical finding (e.g. a 5% reduction in working hours) might be considered evidence of basic income's failure or success depending on one's perspective on work and freedom. This book examines the empirical relationship between welfare mechanisms and job search behaviour without presuming that more job search or work effort is inherently preferable, recognising that varying normative perspectives exist regarding the optimal distribution of work in society.

Basic income experiments are, by their very nature, time limited. The average period for receipt of basic income payments is around 2 years. Critics argue that a two-year duration is too short for meaningful behavioural changes (Gilbert et al., 2018), especially since participants know the payments are temporary (Thorne, 2018). The knowledge that payments will cease after this inevitably impacts on decision making, particularly around labour market behaviour. However, the impact of such knowledge may not be straightforward.

For some, a short term cash injection may not constitute enough motivation or financial incentive to alter paid work patterns. Alternatively, people may take advantage of the defined period of additional income to take a break from work, or reduce their hours, knowing, or at least assuming that, once the experiment ends, their work patterns would return to those prior to the experiment. Certain groups in particular may have a more pronounced effect within a population. For example, young parents may use the short term basic income as means of extending their maternity or paternity leave, thereby reducing short term labour market participation. A short term experiment may therefore inflate the negative labour market impact amongst this group. Unfortunately, there is no data on the post-experiment behaviours of participants to examine this empirically. It is therefore impossible to determine whether the effects of a short term experiment would be replicated if a basic income was fully implemented over the longer term.

Basic income is theorised to have the most pronounced impact on work incentives at the lower end of the income scale. As Widerquist (2018) argues, the impact of a basic income on work incentives diminishes proportionally as household income increases. Understandably, participants from experiments are largely drawn from low income households. However, this focus makes it impossible to extrapolate findings to middle and higher income groups. This creates a significant knowledge gap regarding how basic income might influence labour market behaviour across the full socioeconomic spectrum.

The response of employers to the introduction of basic income and potential changes in labour supply will be crucial to the long term impact of basic income. The iterative relationship between labour supply and demand is key to understanding how basic income may reform labour markets. However, there is little evidence of these phenomena from basic income experiments as very few analyses include a demand response. Both theory and evidence suggest that a decrease in labour supply would lead to higher wages, as employers are forced to increase financial incentives to work, which in turn may prompt an increased labour supply in response to the increased financial incentives to work, resulting in a partial reversal of labour time reduction (Bracha et al., 2015; Pucar & Tolić, 2022; Widerquist, 2018). Only two studies examine labour demand response in basic income experiments. The first examines data from a 'saturation' site in the Manitoba experiment in Canada in the 1970s (Calnitsky, 2020), and the second from the Alaskan permanent dividend (Jones & Marinescu, 2022). Interestingly, they both find an increase in local wages, although in Alaska, this was deemed to be due to increases in consumer demand rather than a fall in working hours. However, more evidence is required to explore the labour demand response in more depth and across different contexts.

In most experiments, recipients of basic income were randomly selected from the population and were therefore spread across the geographic location in which the experiment was set. As a result, there were no interactional effects of basic income at a community level. The only experiments that have included a 'saturation site', where everyone in a town was eligible, were the Mincome and Ontario experiments in Canada. The Ontario experiment was cancelled before sufficient evidence of community effects could be gleaned from it. However, insight from the Mincome experiment suggests a community effect exists, pushing down labour market engagement (Calnitsky & Latner, 2017). Again, this limited evidential base means that more research is required to explore this phenomenon.

The different social, economic, and political contexts in which each experiment occurred must also be considered when drawing conclusions from the findings. Perhaps most important is the fact that the NIT experiments took place over 40 years prior to the other experiments. Labour markets have changed since that time, with several significant trends, including increases in precarious work and female participation.[1] These changes suggest important cultural shifts, which mean that the results from the NIT experiments in the 1970s, whilst instructive, must be recognised within their specific historical context. Identifying these limitations helps to recognise the usefulness of the evidence that such experiments produce. The next section examines the degree to which each experiment examined replicates a basic income.

## Summary of Basic Income Experiments

Table 3.1 is a summary of the main experiments included in the review and sets out how many of the basic income criteria each experiment meets.

The experiments which rank closest to a basic income are two of the 'natural' experiments, the Alaskan permanent dividend, which is only not classed as a basic income due to the fact that it is paid annually at varying rates, and the Cherokee permanent dividend which fails the universal test, although it could be argued that it is universal as it is paid to every member of the Cherokee community. The other 'natural experiment' included is lottery winners who, instead of winning a lump sum, receive their winnings in the form of an annuity, regular payments for the rest of their lives. These are not universal and, indeed, limited to very small sections of the overall population.

The basic income experiments carried out over the last decade or so share many characteristics of basic income, with a particular emphasis on the removal of conditionality, but are neither universal nor permanent. The Negative Income Tax ("NIT") experiments undertaken in the United States and Canada in the 1960s and 1970s differ from the later experiments, being means-tested and based on the household rather than individual.

[1] The overall participation rate of women in the labour market in the US in 1970 was 43% (Toossi, 2002). The participation rate in 2022 was 56.8% (US Labor Statistics, 2023).

**Table 3.1** Summary of basic income experiments in high-income countries

| *Experiment* | *Years* | *Universal* | *Unconditional* | *Individual* | *Not means-tested* | *Non-withdrawable* | *Regular* | *Flat rate* | *Permanent* |
|---|---|---|---|---|---|---|---|---|---|
| Basic income | | ✓ | ✓ | ✓ | ✓ | ✓ | ✓ | ✓ | ✓ |
| Alaska, US | 1982-present | ✓ | ✓ | ✓ | ✓ | ✓ | × | ✓ | ✓ |
| Cherokee,US | 1996-present | × | ✓ | ✓ | ✓ | ✓ | ✓ | ✓ | ✓ |
| Lottery, Belgium, Sweden, US | 2005 | × | ✓ | ✓ | ✓ | ✓ | ✓ | ✓ | ✓ |
| Finland | 2017–18 | × | ✓ | ✓ | ✓ | ✓ | ✓ | ✓ | × |
| Ontario, Canada | 2016–18 | × | ✓ | ✓ | ✓ | ✓ | ✓ | ✓ | × |
| ORUS, US | 2020–23 | × | ✓ | ✓ | ✓ | ✓ | ✓ | ✓ | × |
| PPGIP, US | 2021–23 | × | ✓ | ✓ | ✓ | ✓ | ✓ | ✓ | × |
| Wales, UK | 2022–25 | × | ✓ | ✓ | ✓ | ✓ | ✓ | ✓ | × |
| New Jersey, US | 1968–72 | × | ✓ | × | × | ✓ | ✓ | × | × |
| RIME,US | 1970–72 | × | ✓ | × | × | ✓ | ✓ | × | × |
| SIME/ DIME, US | 1970–80 | × | ✓ | × | × | ✓ | ✓ | × | × |
| Gary, Indiana, US | 1971–74 | × | ✓ | × | × | ✓ | ✓ | × | × |
| Mincome, Canada | 1971–74 | × | ✓ | × | × | ✓ | ✓ | × | × |

(continued)

**Table 3.1** (continued)

| *Experiment* | *Years* | *Universal* | *Unconditional* | *Individual* | *Not means-tested* | *Non-withdrawable* | *Regular* | *Flat rate* | *Permanent* |
|---|---|---|---|---|---|---|---|---|---|
| B-Mincome, Spain | 2016–19 | × | × | × | × | ✓ | ✓ | ✓ | × |
| Weten Wat Werkt, Utrecht, Netherlands | 2018–19 | × | × | × | × | ✓ | ✓ | ✓ | × |

*Sources* Widerquist (2005), Calnitsky et al. (2019), Hoynes and Rothstein (2019), Kangas et al. (2019), Verlaat et al. (2020), McDowell and Ferdosi (2021), Jones and Marinescu (2022), Riutort et al. (2023), Holland et al. (2024), Nichols et al. (2025), Vivalt et al. (2025)

The main difference between basic income and NIT is the payment mechanism. Basic income is paid to everyone who is eligible (i.e. all individuals in a defined political community) regardless of their other wealth or income. It may be taxed away, but it is not means-tested away. In contrast, whilst everyone may be eligible for an NIT, it is means-tested and so not everyone who may be eligible will receive a payment. It guarantees a minimum level of income to those on low incomes, whereas a basic income is paid regardless. Due to this, they only share two of the six dimensions with basic income, being unconditional and regular payments.

The following review is split into four parts, starting with evidence from the 'natural' experiments, the programme in Alaska and the Cherokee programme, together with lottery winners. It then looks at the more recent basic income experiments in Finland, North America, the Netherlands, and Wales and finally the historic Negative Income Tax experiments in North America.

### *Natural Experiments*

Whilst basic income is commonly framed as an alternative form of welfare payment, it has also been positioned as a social dividend, a payment derived from collective economic production to which all should be entitled (Standing, 2019). Both the Alaskan dividend and Cherokee Demogrant are examples of this concept. They have similar funding mechanisms, with the Alaskan dividend being paid out of a sovereign wealth fund established in Alaska in 1976 based on the State's oil wealth. The Cherokee Demogrant is paid out of the profits from casinos on tribal land.

The Alaskan permanent dividend only misses out on being defined as a basic income due to it only being paid once a year, rather than as a 'regular' payment envisaged under basic income, which would be paid weekly or monthly. The average annual payment since 2010 is $1444 per individual, far below a subsistence level income. Although for families it can represent a significant income boost, accounting for up to 20% of annual household income amongst low income households (Hiilamo, 2022).

The impact of the dividends on labour market behaviour is limited. A study on labour supply in 2015 (Jones & Marinescu, 2022) found no evidence of a detrimental effect on total employment at the extensive margin (the number of people working). However, the study did note a decline in overall employment at the intensive margin (the amount people work), with a rise in the number of individuals working part-time. There is no evidence relating to the impact on job search intensity, whilst the impact on work incentives appears to be mixed. When asked about the influence that the dividend had on willingness to do paid work, recipients reported a mixed effect with 21% reporting a positive effect and 16% a negative effect, whilst the majority reported that it had no effect (Harstad, 2017). However, a positive response to attitudinal questions does not appear to relate directly to positive changes in labour market behaviour.

In a similar vein to the Alaskan permanent dividend, The Eastern Cherokee Native American tribe pays a 'Demogrant' to all its adult members, financed by the profits from casinos on tribal lands. Payments began in 1996 and amount to around $4000 per year for every adult tribe member, significantly higher than the dividends paid by the Alaskan scheme. Nevertheless, a study of the impact of the payments found no changes in labour participation following the introduction of the payments (Akee et al., 2010).

Lotteries also represent 'natural' experiments, in which people receive additional unearned income, somewhat akin to a basic income. Certain lottery winnings are paid out as an annuity, with regular payments made throughout the remainder of the winner's life. Winners are fully aware that the payments will continue until they die and are therefore in a position to plan for the longer term, rather than thinking that the income from a basic income will be cut off after two years. However, the sample size of such winners is very small. An analysis of such a lottery, the Belgian 'Win for Life' lottery game (Marx & Peeters, 2008) found small changes in work activity. Whilst almost all winners remained in work, only a small proportion reduced their working hour, suggesting an insignificant impact of lottery winnings on labour market participation.

### *Recent Basic Income Experiments in Europe and North America*

Finland, the Province of Ontario in Canada, various US states, and Wales have all conducted basic income type experiments in recent years. The Finnish experiment between 2016 and 2018 sought to examine whether a basic income would act as an incentive to move the long term unemployed back into work, focusing on creating greater incentives to work and reducing bureaucracy (Kangas et al., 2021). Basic income was viewed as a pragmatic way of getting people back into work by addressing mechanisms identified as barriers to employment (De Wispelaere et al., 2019).

The experiment focused solely on unemployed individuals. This population was perceived as more responsive to the implementation of a basic income resulting from multiple disincentives to work caused by high marginal tax rates as well as administrative hurdles on moving back into work. The experiment was conducted to determine if the elimination of these barriers would increase participation in the labour market (Kangas et al., 2019). Unlike other experiments, which examined changes amongst those already in work, the Finland experiment provides useful insight into the impact of a basic income on the unemployed.

The main measure of work incentive was the number of days worked at the beginning of the experiment compared to the number of days after each year of the two year experiment (Kangas et al., 2021). The average number of days employed during the experiment period did not significantly differ between the basic income and control groups. According to the findings, receiving basic income did not significantly contribute to finding employment (Kangas et al., 2021). However, basic income recipients did show a higher tendency towards part-time employment compared to the control group, which may have been driven, at least to some degree, by the financial guarantee provided by basic income. There are additional findings from the experiment which are of broader interest to those examining basic income.

Contrary to expectations, many members of the basic income group continued to make use of employment services and active labour market policy measures (ALMP) voluntarily (Hiilamo, 2022), despite the behavioural conditions attached to their usage, including job search requirements. This finding suggests that most recipients did not necessarily object to the conditionality of employment services (Hiilamo, 2022), and/or they viewed the efficacy of such services as more important than the negative impacts of the behavioural conditions. This finding runs counter to assumed behaviour, and other empirical evidence, where it is expected that, given the choice, unemployed people would avoid being subject to behavioural conditions where possible.

In addition to directly measured employment outcomes, the Finnish experiment also used survey data asking respondents to evaluate their employment 'possibilities' within the coming year. Those in receipt of basic income displayed greater confidence in their re-employment opportunities compared to the control group (69% and 56% respectively), indicating a significant empowerment effect of basic income (Kangas et al., 2021).

The Ontario Basic Income Pilot (OBIP) launched in 2014 with around 4000 recipients, including a 2000 person 'saturation' site in the town of Lindsey to study community effects. Unlike the Finnish experiment, which focused on employment outcomes, the Ontario pilot was borne out of the ruling Liberal Party's strategy to reduce poverty (McDowell & Ferdosi, 2021). Compared to other experiments, OBIP paid a relatively generous basic income, higher than existing social assistance payments but still below the poverty threshold. They nevertheless constituted significant increases for those on low incomes compared to existing benefits which they were designed to replace (McDowell & Ferdosi, 2021). OBIP was due to last for two years, but a change in government saw the experiment abruptly cancelled in 2018, meaning that most participants received payments for less than 17 months. The cancellation disrupted both recipients' longer term planning, with 95% of survey respondents reportedly abandoning life plans as a result of the cancellation (McDowell & Ferdosi, 2021), as well as the opportunity for collecting research data. Findings that did emerge showed labour market participation decreased amongst those in employment at the beginning of the experiment, whilst 85% of those unemployed at the beginning remained so, though the majority cited health as a significant barrier to employment (Hamilton & Mulvale, 2019).

Qualitative data revealed that basic income made job hunting easier for two thirds of working and one third of jobless recipients. It also supported long term financial planning, as well as encouraging participation in education and training. Many basic income recipients also felt that traditional welfare programmes discouraged work through behavioural conditions that required bureaucratic tasks and high marginal tax rates when taking on paid work (Hamilton & Mulvale, 2019).

Two of the many recent guaranteed income experiments in the United States present a somewhat contradictory picture of how cash transfers affect labour market behaviour. ORUS took place across two US states, Illinois and Texas, paying 1000 low income individuals $1000 per month for three years. PGIP was located in a single city, Providence in Rhode Island, and paid a smaller sample of 110 low income individuals $500 dollars a month for 18 months. ORUS resulted in modest reductions in labour supply, with participants working 1–2 hours fewer per week (a 4–5% reduction) and experienced longer unemployment spells. Notably, findings suggest that recipients engaged in more selective job search behaviour, applying for fewer positions. However, the study found no measurable improvements in job quality or wages (Vivalt et al., 2025). In contrast, findings from PGIP showed that recipients experienced larger increases in full-time employment, compared to the control group. The evaluation of the programme found that recipients used the increased financial stability offered by the payments to look for more dignified and better paid work, balancing work with personal wellbeing (Nichols et al., 2025).

Findings from both experiments suggest that recipients made use of the increased financial security afforded by payments to re-consider their relationships with paid work, particularly in the aftermath of the COVID-19 pandemic, which caused significant economic disruption. Some participants prioritised increased leisure time, whilst others spent more time in family and caring responsibilities or looked for work which was better aligned to their values and needs. There is some evidence of increased educational enrolment amongst younger participants, suggesting longer term planning. The divergent labour market outcomes between the two experiments highlights the importance of context when considering the potential impact of basic income. Of particular relevance may be the significant differences in the levels of payments and their duration, with ORUS paying twice as much as PGIP and for twice as long. However, we can only surmise that such differences were significant without evidence to link these factors.

In 2022, Wales launched a basic income experiment for care leavers aged 18 and over to address the significant barriers young people face during the transition to adulthood. The experiment was originally due to run until 2027 but was shortened to 2025 due to the costs involved (Walesonline, 2023). 635 participants each receive unconditional payments of £1600 (£1280 after the deduction of tax) each month. This constitutes a generous basic income payment, equivalent to the real Living Wage, for an employee working full-time (livingwage.org.uk). Payments are therefore much higher than the payments or guarantee levels in other experiments[2] (Holland et al., 2024), potentially creating significant disincentives to work amongst recipients. This concern was raised by professionals involved with the care leavers, who feared that basic income could disincentivise education, training and employment amongst recipients (Holland et al., 2024).

However, young participants' experiences undermine these fears as many reported that the basic income allowed them to explore different educational or employment options that better align with their interests, whilst providing financial security that enabled them to make longer term decisions. Notably, recipients consistently attributed unemployment to a lack of employment opportunities, rather than diminished motivation to find work (Mathur et al., 2025). Other professionals also provided evidence of young people continuing or going back to education, training, and employment, with specific examples highlighting choices to re-train in more desirable careers and participants moving away from precarious, zero-hours contracts into more sustainable jobs, which the evaluation of the pilot describes as 'future or goal-oriented decisions' (Holland et al., 2024). The latest evaluation of the pilot concludes that findings provide some support to the argument that basic income provides recipients with the power to say 'no' to unfavourable jobs and instead focus on finding the work they want to do. However, the evaluation cautions against ascribing this power based on preliminary short term findings (Mathur et al., 2025).

### *Historic Negative Income Tax Experiments in North America*

Of all the main basic income type experiments, most has been written about the Negative Income Tax 'NIT' experiments in North America in the 1960s and early 1970s, which have spawned over 200 books and articles (Widerquist, 2005, 2019), with interpretation of the results described as a 'political Rorschach test' revealing more about who is making the claims than the results themselves (Widerquist, 2005).

The experiments sought to explore the potential impact of implementing an NIT, targeting low income households. The NITs were

[2] The payments equivalent to £15,360 per year before tax, are higher than the relative poverty threshold of 60% median income for a single person with no children: £11,804 (https://observatory.leeds.gov.uk/leeds-poverty-fact-book/relative-and-absolute-poverty/).

unconditional and paid irrespective of working status, but unlike basic income, they were based on the family/household rather than paid to each individual. The aim of the NIT experiments was to assess the effects of an income guarantee on labour supply, investigating the extent to which work effort would decrease if people were assured a minimum income (Levine et al., 2017) and to test whether the expected negative impact on hours in paid work would be small enough to justify their sustainability as a means of reducing poverty amongst low income households (Widerquist, 2019).

Overall, the NIT experiments showed small decreases in labour market participation across demographic groups, with more significant decreases amongst those who are not the main earner in a household. Evidence points to some specific reasons for reducing labour market participation, including caring commitments and health issues, as well as the potential for an increase in reservation wages, lending support to the argument that basic income enables people to say no to poorly paid work. However, as Widerquist (2019) points out in relation to the North American NITs, the rise and fall of labour hours tends to mirror the health of the overall economy. His conclusion is that, when better jobs were available, both those receiving basic income (treatment groups) and those not (control groups) took them up. However, when fewer good jobs were available, the control group, lacking the same financial support as the treatment group, continued to search for and take on less attractive jobs (Widerquist, 2005). Work reduction may therefore be largely attributed to timing issues, with recipients of NIT/basic income taking more time to find their next job than those who did not receive payments. This reflects a problem in the way that findings are reported solely in terms of hours worked over a set period of time but do not reflect the longer term implications of taking longer to find a more suitable job.

## Recommendations for Future Basic Income Experiments

Short term experiments cannot fully capture longer term impacts on labour market, particularly the iterative inter-relations between labour supply and demand, each of which will inevitably shift, based on changes in the other. The targeted, short timescales of experiments, and focus on specific sub-populations, limit our ability to make conclusions about longer term impacts of basic income.

Whilst acknowledging that all experiments are constrained by financial, political, and legal factors, this section provides a 'wish list' of priorities for future basic income experiments.

1. **Comprehensive analysis of job search activities.** An examination of job search behaviour in addition to labour market participation, focusing on job search activities, whether and how these change from pre-basic income, and changes in job preferences over time, both in terms of the nature of the work and changes in preferences between full- and part-time working patterns.
2. **Longer timeframes.** Two years is not a long enough period to capture potential changes in relationships between employees and employers. Longer experiments would help distinguish between short term and long term responses and behavioural changes.
3. **Labour demand response analysis.** To fully understand the impact of basic income, we need to understand responses of both labour supply and demand, which will be iterative. Changes in one will likely lead to changes in the other.
4. **Diverse demographic representation.** Experiments should deliberately include varied demographic groups, including households higher up the income/wealth scale, to gain a better understanding of how basic income interacts with factors including gender, age, education level, family structure, and socioeconomic status.
5. **Saturation sites.** Basic income experiments need to be conducted in areas where all residents are eligible for payments. Only by doing this can they assess what Calnitsky and Latner (2017) describe as 'community effects', where interactions between members of a community who all receive basic income will re-shape the labour market and social norms around paid work.

Incorporating these recommendations into future experiments would enable them to fill critical gaps in our knowledge and provide more robust evidence on how basic income may transform both job search activities and interaction with the labour market more broadly.

## Lessons Learned: Synthesising Experimental Findings for Policy and Practice

Evidence from basic income experiments across a range of contexts reveals broadly consistent patterns in labour market effects. Most experiments show small reductions in labour market participation, primarily at the intensive margin (hours worked), rather than the extensive margin (the number of people in work). Some experiments identified increases in the number of people in part-time work, suggesting that basic income enables people to balance their work and other responsibilities more effectively. More recent experiments have also identified increased sense of self-efficacy in relation to the labour market. Table 3.2 summarises the main findings from each experiment or programme in relation to labour market behaviours.

Experiments conducted across diverse contexts have consistently yielded similar results, suggesting their findings provide a useful indication of some of the effects that may take shape under basic income. There is evidence of small reductions in the amount of paid work undertaken, although no large scale desertion of the labour market has been detected. Even with a relatively high basic income, results from Ontario suggest that overall decreases in paid work are small. The labour demand in response to decreases is harder to measure, although what little evidence there is indicates that employers may respond to reductions in labour supply with increased wages to attract workers, which could offset initial decreases in labour supply over time, although this cannot be empirically proven by short term experiments.

Whilst the evidence base on labour market participation grows, understanding of basic income's effects on job search behaviour remains underdeveloped. Extrapolating from existing evidence from the basic income experiments, it appears that the removal of conditionality has limited impact on job search intensity overall but may enable more selective approaches. For example, in Finland, many recipients continued to make use of employment services and ALMPs, despite the lack of compulsion. In Ontario, recipients reported using the additional financial security offered by basic income to search for more suitable employment.

The next chapter introduces the methodological framework that underpins the empirical analysis in this book. It explains how Qualitative Comparative Analysis (QCA) serves as a bridge between theoretical

**Table 3.2** Summary of labour market outcomes

| *Name* | *Labour market behaviour* | | *Work incentive* |
|---|---|---|---|
| | *Extensive margin* | *Intensive margin* | |
| Alaskan Permanent Dividend | No change | Small reduction | Mixed—mostly no effect |
| Cherokee Demogrant | No change | No change | No data |
| Finland Basic Income | No change | Small increase in part-time work | Increase—higher confidence in finding work |
| Ontario Basic Income Pilot | Small reduction | Small reduction | Increase—job hunting made simpler |
| Wales Basic Income for Care Leavers | Mixed effects | Mixed effects | Increase—more goal-oriented decisions |
| ORUS (US) | Small reduction | Small reduction (1–2 hrs/week) | No data |
| PGIP (US) | Increase in full-time employment | Increase | Increase—looked for better paid work |
| North American NITs | Small reduction | Small reduction | No data |
| Lottery Winners | Small reduction | Small reduction | No data |
| B-Mincome (Spain) | Small reduction | Small reduction—decreased full-time work with permanent contracts | Increase—improved mental bandwidth and positive thoughts about employment possibilities |
| Weten Wat Werkt (Netherlands) | Mixed effects—varies by intervention group | Mixed effects—positive results for small jobs | Increase—higher self-efficacy in "Autonomously in action" and "Extra help" groups |

concepts of basic income and the analysis of existing welfare regimes, outlining the key principles of QCA, including set theory, calibration processes, and methods for identifying necessary and sufficient conditions for outcomes. It shows how fuzzy-set ideal type analysis enables systematic comparisons to be made between theoretical basic income principles and existing welfare policies, whilst fuzzy-set QCA helps uncover the causal relationships between welfare configurations and job search behaviours.

This methodological approach provides the foundation for examining how closely current European welfare regimes align with basic income principles and their effects on unemployment.

## References


Akee, R. K., Copeland, W. E., Keeler, G., Angold, A., & Costello, E. J. (2010). Parents' incomes and children's outcomes: A quasi-experiment using transfer payments from casino profits. *American Economic Journal: Applied Economics, 2*(1), 86–115.

Bracha, A., Gneezy, U., & Loewenstein, G. (2015). Relative pay and labor supply. *Journal of Labor Economics, 33*(2), 297–315. https://doi.org/10.1086/678494

Calnitsky, D. (2020). The employer response to the guaranteed annual income. *Socio-Economic Review, 18*(2), 493–517.

Calnitsky, D., & Latner, J. P. (2017). Basic income in a small town: Understanding the elusive effects on work. *Social Problems, 64*(3), 373–397.

Calnitsky, D., Latner, J. P., & Forget, E. L. (2019). Life after work: The impact of basic income on nonemployment activities. *Social Science History, 43*(4), 657–677.

De Wispelaere, J., Halmetoja, A., & Pulkka, V.-V. (2019). The Finnish basic income experiment: A primer. In M. Torry (Ed.), *The Palgrave international handbook of basic income* (pp. 389–406). Springer International Publishing (Exploring the Basic Income Guarantee). https://doi.org/10.1007/978-3-030-23614-4_20

Gilbert, R., et al. (2018). Would a basic income guarantee reduce the motivation to work? An Analysis of labor responses in 16 trial programs. *Basic Income Studies, 13*, 2. https://doi.org/10.1515/bis-2018-0011

Hamilton, L., & Mulvale, J. P. (2019). "Human again": The (unrealized) promise of basic income in Ontario. *Journal of Poverty, 23*(7), 576–599. https://doi.org/10.1080/10875549.2019.1616242

Harstad, P. (2017). "Executive Summary of Findings from a Survey of Alaska Voters on the PFD". *Harstad Strategic Research.* Accessed June, 11, 2024.

Hiilamo, H. (2022). Lessons from basic income experiments. In *Participation Income*. Edward Elgar Publishing, pp. 51–82. Retrieved January 27, 2024, from https://www.elgaronline.com/monochap-oa/book/9781800880801/book-part-9781800880801-12.xml

Holland, S., et al. (2024). Basic income for care leavers in Wales pilot evaluation: Annual report, 2023 to 2024. Retrieved April 20, 2024, from https://orca.cardiff.ac.uk/id/eprint/166856/

Hoynes, H., & Rothstein, J. (2019). Universal basic income in the United States and advanced countries. *Annual Review of Economics, 11*(1), 929–958. https://doi.org/10.1146/annurev-economics-080218-030237

Jones, D., & Marinescu, I. (2022). The labor market impacts of universal and permanent cash transfers: Evidence from the Alaska Permanent Fund. *American Economic Journal: Economic Policy, 14*(2), 315–340.

Kangas, O., et al. (2019). *The basic income experiment 2017–2018 in Finland: Preliminary results*. Retrieved February 9, 2024, from https://julkaisut.valtioneuvosto.fi/handle/10024/161361

Kangas, O., et al. (2021). *Experimenting with unconditional basic income: Lessons from the Finnish BI experiment 2017–2018*. Edward Elgar Publishing. Retrieved February 7, 2024, from https://books.google.com/books?hl=en&lr=&id=d3g8EAAAQBAJ&oi=fnd&pg=PR1&dq=Experimenting+with+Unconditional+Basic+Income:+Lessons+from+the+Finnish+BI+...&ots=TOiHW1qqm5&sig=V_cSv1zIVC4jCNSNQxqho7yx8vQ

Levine, R.A., et al. (2017). A retrospective on the negative income tax experiments: Looking back at the most innovate field studies in social policy. In *The ethics and economics of the basic income guarantee* (pp. 95–106). Routledge. Retrieved February 11, 2024, from https://www.taylorfrancis.com/chapters/edit/10.4324/9781315239934-5/retrospective-negative-income-tax-experiments-looking-back-innovate-field-studies-social-policy-robert-levine-harold-watts-robinson-hollister-walter-williams-alice-connor-karl-widerquist

Marx, A., & Peeters, H. (2008). An unconditional basic income and labor supply: Results from a pilot study of lottery winners. *The Journal of Socio-Economics, 37*(4), 1636–1659.

Mathur, V., Roberts, L., Bezeczky, Z., Lloyd, H., Vallis, D., Sanders, M., ... & Westlake, D. (2025). Basic income for care leavers in Wales pilot evaluation: Second annual report, 2024 to 2025.

McDowell, T., & Ferdosi, M. (2021). The Impacts of the Ontario basic income pilot: A comparative analysis of the findings from the Hamilton region. *Basic Income Studies, 16*(2), 209–256. https://doi.org/10.1515/bis-2020-0034

Neuwinger, M. (2022). The revolution will not be randomized: Universal basic income, randomized controlled trials, and "evidence-based" social policy. *Global Social Policy, 22*(1), 27–45. https://doi.org/10.1177/14680181211010102

Nichols, B., et al. (2025). *The American Guaranteed Income Studies: Providence, Rhode Island*. Centre for Guaranteed Income Research, Social Policy & Practice, University of Pennsylvania.

Pucar, S., & Tolić, I. (2022). The intensity of impact of labor supply reduction onto the growth of wages In Republic Of Srpska. *EMC Review-Economy and Market Communication Review, 23*(1), 136–148.

Riutort, S., Laín, B., & Julià, A. (2023). Basic income at municipal level: Insights from the Barcelona B-MINCOME Pilot. *Basic Income Studies, 18*(1), 1–30. https://doi.org/10.1515/bis-2021-0047

Standing, G. (2019). Plunder of the commons: A manifesto for sharing public wealth. Penguin UK.

Thorne, M. (2018). Testing time: Uncovering potential impacts of project duration in basic income pilots. Retrieved April 21, 2024, from https://openresearch.ocadu.ca/id/eprint/2264/

Toossi, M. (2002). A century of change: The US labor force, 1950–2050. *Monthly Labor Review, 125*, 15.

Van Parijs, P. (1992). Arguing for Basic income. *Ethical Foundations for a Radical reform*. https://dial.uclouvain.be/pr/boreal/object/boreal:96711

Verlaat, T., et al. (2020). *Study what works (Weten wat werkt)*. Utrecht University.

Vivalt, E., et al. (2025). NBER working paper series.

Walesonline (2023). https://www.walesonline.co.uk/news/politics/wales-not-continue-paying-care-27990859

Widerquist, K. (2005). A failure to communicate: What (if anything) can we learn from the negative income tax experiments? *The Journal of Socio-Economics, 34*(1), 49–81.

Widerquist, K. (2018). *A critical analysis of basic income experiments for researchers, policymakers, and citizens*. Springer International Publishing. https://doi.org/10.1007/978-3-030-03849-6

Widerquist, K. (2019). The negative income tax experiments of the 1970s. In: M. Torry (Ed.) *The Palgrave international handbook of basic income* (pp. 303–318). Springer International Publishing (Exploring the Basic Income Guarantee). https://doi.org/10.1007/978-3-030-23614-4_15.

CHAPTER 4

# Using Qualitative Comparative Analysis (QCA) in Social Policy Research

**Abstract** Chapter four provides an overview of qualitative comparative analysis (QCA), the methodological approach used in this book. QCA is a valuable analytical tool for cross-country analysis and enables nuanced, comparative analysis of international welfare regimes. The chapter sets out the main characteristics of QCA as a methodological approach and how it acts as a bridge between theory and empirical analysis, which is essential when considering the potential effects of basic income. It sets out the key concepts used in QCA and how they will be used later in this book. This methodological bridge between theory and empirical analysis allows a systematic examination of how basic income principles manifest in real-world welfare systems, setting up the foundation for later analysis of their effects on job search behaviour.

**Keywords** Set theory · Causal complexity · Fuzzy sets · Calibration · Ideal types · Necessity and sufficiency · Counterfactual analysis

QCA is a powerful tool for understanding how welfare policies function across different institutional contexts. This chapter introduces QCA, a methodological approach that bridges the gap between theory and empirical research in social policy studies. It offers unique advantages for



S. Watkins, *Basic Income, Work Incentives and Job Search Behaviour*, Exploring the Basic Income Guarantee,
https://doi.org/10.1007/978-3-031-99197-4_4

cross-country analysis and comparative studies of welfare systems, making it particularly valuable for examining complex policy interventions like basic income (Befani, 2016; Blackman et al., 2013; Hanckel et al., 2021). Understanding how basic income principles operate within diverse welfare contexts requires a methodological approach that can capture complexity, nuance, and variation. (QCA) offers a powerful lens for this purpose, allowing researchers to explore how different configurations of conditions relate to particular outcomes across multiple cases. By drawing on set theory and allowing for both conceptual clarity and empirical instances, QCA makes it possible to systematically compare welfare regimes and assess the extent to which they align with or diverge from basic income principles.

## Key Concepts in QCA

QCA is grounded in complexity theory; it recognises that outcomes are often produced by combinations of conditions (Befani, 2013). As such, it is capable of handling complex, multifaceted phenomena where the interaction of conditions, rather than single conditions in isolation, lead to particular outcomes (Ragin, 2009a). It also recognises that there may be multiple paths to the same outcome (Rihoux & Ragin, 2008), demonstrating that in complex systems, multiple and diverse causes or combinations of conditions can lead to the same outcome. QCA combines formalised comparison with a strong emphasis on the individuality and complexity of cases (Oana, Schneider & Thomann, 2021), facilitating comparisons across cases and contexts, which is central to the analysis within this book.

QCA is capable of incorporating both quantitative and qualitative data, integrating 'the best features of the case-oriented approach with the best features of the variable-oriented approach' (Ragin, 1987, p. 84), making it a versatile method, adaptable to a variety of research settings and capable of answering a range of questions. This methodological approach rests on a number of key concepts, which are set out below.

### *Causal Complexity*

Social policies operate within complex institutional environments where multiple factors interact. Causal complexity acknowledges that social outcomes rarely stem from single, isolated causes but emerge from different combinations of conditions that vary across contexts.

In studying basic income, this complexity is particularly relevant. The same policy intervention may produce different outcomes depending on the existing welfare regime, labour market regulations, social norms around paid work, and economic conditions. Causal complexity enables analysis of how basic income principles might function across diverse welfare regimes through three characteristics:

- Equifinality—refers to the possibility that there may be separate, non-mutually exclusive explanations for the same phenomenon.
- Conjunctural causation—where the effects of a single condition can only be seen when combined with other conditions.
- Causal asymmetry—describes the way in which insights on the causal role of a condition help to explain the presence of an outcome but is of little use in explaining its absence. (Mahoney, 2008; Ragin, 2014).

The combination of equifinality, conjunctural causation, and causal asymmetry enables QCA to capture the impact of conditions that are difficult to capture using quantitative methods. Causal asymmetry describes the way in which insights on the causal role of a condition help to explain the presence of an outcome but is of little use in explaining its absence.

Context is an important concept in QCA. The use of specifically chosen cases to include in the analysis effectively sets a limit on defined empirical contexts within which the insights gained can be deemed valid (Mahoney & Goertz, 2006). This type of generalisation is referred to as limited, historical, or contingent (Berg-Schlosser et al., 2009; Blatter & Blume, 2008; Rihoux & Ragin, 2008a). The findings from this book are therefore not generalisable beyond the scope of the cases included in the analysis. As a result, this book does not make grand claims about the potential impact of basic income across a range of countries or contexts and limits its inferences to those countries included in the analysis.

### *Set Theory and Set Membership*

Set theory is based on the principle that empirical phenomena can be categorised as a member of a particular set, based on its characteristics and defining principles of set membership (Ragin, 2009b). A simple example is EU membership. If we define EU membership in set theoretical terms, set membership would mean membership of the EU, and non-membership will mean non-membership of the EU set. In set theoretical terms, membership is ascribed with a score of 1 and non-membership a score of 0. In this example there is a clear 'cut off' point between set membership and non-membership.

In the above example, each country included in the analysis of EU members represents a 'case'. A case is like a variable used in quantitative research, but rather than having a single dimension, such as population or GDP, a case can encapsulate a range of dimensions. In QCA analysis, cases are carefully chosen to represent different combinations of important features. Each case in this book represents a unique mix of policy characteristics that may help explain why certain outcomes occur. For example, the analysis examines how different welfare regimes combine features like conditionality and universalism, then observes how these combinations relate to outcomes, specifically job search behaviour.

After identifying the relevant characteristics, cases are systematically compared to discover meaningful patterns. This comparison isn't always straightforward, as cases can be classified in different ways depending on the researcher's perspective. The process of determining whether a case is a member of a set is called calibration, an iterative process that is at the core of set theory, moving back and forth between theory and evidence to establish 'qualitative cut off' points between set members and non-members. These classification decisions significantly impact the analysis, so researchers must clearly document their calibration choices and reasoning. This transparency allows others to understand how sets were constructed and evaluate the validity of the classifications.

### *Crisp and Fuzzy Sets*

When examining social phenomena, the distinction between set membership and non-membership may not be immediately clear, which is why two ways of measuring membership of sets have been developed: crisp and fuzzy. Crisp sets have only two distinct states: membership and non-membership. Returning to the EU example, in crisp terms there are only two possible states: membership and non-membership. A country is either a member of the EU or not. There is no partial membership. However, many phenomena of interest in the social world vary by level or degree, or by quantitative state, as well as qualitative state (Rihoux & Ragin, 2008).

'Crisp' set membership may therefore restrict in depth analysis, removing nuance and reducing membership to a binary, when it is more commonly a scale.

Fuzzy set membership offers a more nuanced measure than simple binary set membership, where partial membership of a set is possible. If we extend the EU membership example, using fuzzy set membership could provide a more nuanced look at EU membership to determine the degree to which countries are either members or not. Such an analysis could consider different elements of EU membership, such as whether they use the Euro as their currency and whether they are members of policies and agreements such as Schengen, which enables people in Member states to cross borders without checks. The use of fuzzy sets could also enable analysis of countries who are not EU members to determine which countries have close ties to the EU and which do not. It could do this by looking at membership of other European organisations, such as the European Economic Area (EEA). Where crisp sets have membership scores of either 1 or 0, fuzzy set membership scores can be anywhere between, and including, 1 and 0. This enables a far more nuanced analysis to be undertaken, although such nuance is accompanied by increased methodological complexity. It is also important to note that, despite the name, fuzzy sets should not be considered fuzzy in the sense of being either ambiguous or imprecise. They require accurate design, based on theoretical concepts and analytical constructs given precise meaning by the researcher making use of them (Kvist, 2007).

### *Determining Set Membership Through Calibration*

Calibration is the process of determining set membership. Sets represent concepts and have boundaries which distinguish between cases that are representative of the concept and those that are not. The primary objective of calibration is to provide an accurate representation of theoretical propositions which can be transposed onto empirical instances to determine the nature and degree of set membership for each case (Verkuilen, 2005). The establishment of boundaries in QCA is known as calibration. The process of calibration uses qualitative 'cut off' points to determine set membership. There are three such cut off points when establishing set membership, the cut off point for full membership (equal to a score of 1), full non-membership (a score of 0), and the cut off point between membership and non-membership, (a score of 0.50). This means that the case is neither in the set, nor out of it, and is hence described as the point of maximum uncertainty for set membership.

A fundamental principle of calibration is that assignment of set memberships should be based on a synthesis of theoretical knowledge and empirical evidence that encompasses a wider range than just the data included in the model (Ragin, 2000). It is advisable to avoid using measurements such as the mean or median in calibrating unless they can be substantiated by theoretical or case knowledge. Nevertheless, the distribution of raw data should not be ignored, and unprocessed data is important in the process of calibration. The determination of set membership scores during the calibration process is also heavily contingent upon the specific study environment (Ragin, 2009a), as the same data may well be transformed into distinct groupings according to different conceptual frameworks. For example, calibrating a set containing 'high per-capita GDP countries' where the population of interest is European countries may require different cut off points to a population of Sub-Saharan Countries even though the same data and measurement are used in both. Set membership scores are therefore limited to the specific study context in which they are used (Schneider & Wagemann, 2012), and cannot be used as universally applicable markers (Collier, 1998).

The cut off point between membership and non-membership in a fuzzy set is a qualitatively anchored point, in contrast to variable-oriented analysis, which is anchored by an empirically derived measure of central tendency, for example the mean. The qualitative anchors used in QCA in effect distinguish between relevant and irrelevant variation, challenging the idea that all variation is meaningful (Ragin, 2000). Returning to the example of calibrating per-capita GDP if, for example the cut off point for being fully in the high GDP set was $20,000, then it would not matter if a country's GDP was $30,000 or $100,000. For the purposes of set membership both cases would score 1, meaning that the research sees no relevant difference between the two figures.

The calibration of sets using fuzzy set analysis gives rise to partial set membership, which is where a case scores between 0 and 1. A partial set membership score denotes both the case's membership score in a set and its antithesis. For example, the next chapter measures welfare conditionality along with its antithesis, unconditionality. As part of the QCA process, each country is assigned a fuzzy set score in the conditional set, which also tells us about its score in the unconditional set. As discussed in chapter four, Germany's score in the conditional set is

0.60, as its score is above the 0.50 cut off point for membership. This means that it is qualitatively a member of the conditional set. It's score in the unconditional set is therefore 0.40 (1.00–0.60). This means that it is neither fully conditional nor unconditional but is more conditional than unconditional, containing elements of both sets. The recognition of cases containing elements of both a condition and its antithesis is an important element in QCA, enabling researchers to distinguish between qualitative and quantitative differences.

QCA measures can consist of single, quantitative measures, for example, per-capita GDP. However, they can also consist of a number of secondary level measures, which may be quantitative, qualitative, or a combination of both. To enable this level of complexity in measures, a variety of approaches have been developed that allow researchers to combine measures or sets to form an overall score for a concept. For example, the measure of conditionality developed in chapter four consists of three secondary level measures: behavioural requirements, monitoring, and sanctions. The measures combine qualitative and quantitative data to determine set membership scores for each secondary level measure. It then combines these sets, using one of three approaches to determine the overall set membership scores for the conditional set (Schneider & Wagemann, 2012):

1. The classical approach. This approach stipulates that all secondary level conditions must be present for the presence of the condition, and therefore for set membership. Using the example of conditionality, the classical approach means that a case would have to be a member of each secondary level measure, behavioural requirements, monitoring, and sanctions, to also be classed as a member of the overall conditional set. This is the most stringent means of combining sets, placing a high bar for overall set membership.
2. The substitutability approach, where the presence of only one of the secondary level conditions would be necessary for the presence of the overall measure. Using this approach, a case would only need to be a member of one of the conditionality secondary level measures to be classed as a member of the conditional set. This is the least stringent means of combining sets, making it easy for cases to be classed as members of the overall set.
3. The family resemblance approach requires the presence of a majority of secondary level conditions as sufficient for membership of the

conditional set. Under this approach, cases can combine any two of the three secondary level measures to be classed as a member of the conditional set. This approach recognises that there may be multiple combinations of factors that can result in overall case membership.

### *Limited Diversity*

Limited diversity refers to instances where there are gaps in empirical examples (Ragin, 2009c). This is of particular interest to QCA as an approach which uses empirical examples as the basis for analysis. In the first instance, QCA relies on empirical examples to analyse the relationship between conditions and outcomes. However, a common problem, which extends to methodologies beyond QCA, is that it is not possible to observe all possible configurations of empirical examples in the real world. This is an issue which specifically impacts on the research in this book, as there is no empirical example of basic income on which to base the analysis. QCA helps to address limited diversity through counterfactual analysis, carefully considering what outcome these unobserved combinations might produce.

Whilst some critics argue this involves mere speculation about non-existent cases (Markoff, 1990; Romme, 1995), proponents maintain it's a strength of QCA as it forces researchers to be explicit about theoretical assumptions and enables insights beyond just observed cases (Ragin, 2014). This approach matches how researchers naturally think about cases—comparing what is observed to what could theoretically exist, whilst maintaining rigour by only using plausible combinations that don't contradict empirical evidence.

In the absence of empirical examples of a fully implemented basic income, this book employs counterfactual thinking, based on theory, the QCA findings, and comparative evidence to examine how basic income might function across different institutional contexts.

## Ideal Types and Fuzzy Set Ideal Type Analysis

The ideal type is a conceptual framework that helps explain social phenomena by creating an exaggerated model based on its 'ideal types'. The construct does not necessarily represent empirical instances of a phenomenon but highlights the most extreme possible versions. Ideal type analysis is used to emphasise particular aspects of reality in their 'purest' forms or to contrast and compare real-world situations, enabling researchers to classify types rather than just rank empirical phenomena (Hudson & Kühner, 2013).

The goal of ideal type analysis is not to describe reality exactly, but rather to help researchers get a deeper knowledge of certain characteristics of a phenomenon by emphasising key elements. This approach is especially helpful for analysing the degree to which existing instances correspond to theoretical concepts (Kvist, 2007), which makes it particularly helpful when examining a theoretical construct like basic income, which naturally contains ideal types of welfare principles including unconditionality, universalism, and individualism. Although it does not exist in the real world, it can be mapped in ideal type terms and compared to real life welfare regimes to measure their resemblance to an ideal type basic income.

The analysis in subsequent chapters uses fuzzy set ideal type analysis ("fsITA") to develop a new ideal type welfare regime based on the principles of basic income, which will help to identify the extent to which countries' welfare regimes approximate basic income.

Fuzzy set ideal type analysis (fsITA) was developed for use in comparative studies, which help to identify differences in both kind and degree (Kvist, 2007). FsITA enables researchers to differentiate between kinds of cases, e.g. those that are conditional and those that are not, as well as degrees of difference, e.g. the extent to which a case is a member of the conditional set, from being only just in the set to being a full member.

There are four main steps in developing an ideal type:

1. Using theory and substantial knowledge to identify sets, e.g. the conditional and unconditional sets used in this book.
2. Calibrating case membership for each of the sets, establishing qualitative cut off points between membership and non-membership of sets, as well as cut off points for full non-membership and full membership.
3. Calculating membership scores for each case in the ideal type model, giving each case a score between 0 (full non-membership of a set) and 1 (full membership of a set, representing an ideal type case).
4. Assessing the cases to gauge how closely each case resembles an ideal, typical instance.

## Fuzzy Set Qualitative Comparative Analysis

The second use of QCA in this book is a causal analysis of the conditions identified in the ideal type analysis as potential mechanisms of change, examining whether these causal conditions are either necessary or sufficient for the presence of two outcomes, high job search intensity and low job search intensity.

QCA is an iterative process, moving back and forth between theory and evidence to identify causal relations (Hudson & Kühner, 2013; Ragin, 2000). For an outcome to have meaning it must be explainable, in relation to theoretical underpinnings. This is achieved using case studies of particular countries following the initial QCA analysis. The purpose of the case studies is to attempt to identify causal mechanisms underpinning the findings of the QCA, to enhance understanding of the causal relations and the specific areas of welfare policy that may have the most impact on job search behaviour.

The final part of the QCA analysis involves counterfactual analysis. Based on theory, previous empirical evidence and the findings of the research in this book, the counterfactual analysis takes two specific countries and conducts a 'thought experiment' on how the introduction of a basic income might impact on job search behaviour and the labour market more broadly, encompassing both labour supply and demand responses to a basic income.

### *Necessity and Sufficiency*

The aim of a QCA is to identify different combinations of causally relevant conditions linked to an outcome (Ragin et al., 2008). It does this by establishing 'necessary' and 'sufficient' conditions for the presence of an outcome of interest, based on an analysis of cases (Rihoux & Ragin, 2008). In QCA, a necessary condition is one that must be present for the outcome to be present. A sufficient condition is one that can exist in isolation for the outcome to be present, but which is not necessary for it to be present.

The analysis of necessary conditions seeks to establish whether a single condition, or configuration of conditions, is necessary to produce the outcome. The basic logic of necessity is that a condition is said to be necessary for the outcome if, whenever the outcome is present, so is the condition. The condition can be seen as a subset of the outcome.

In necessity terms, there may be cases that demonstrate the condition but not the outcome, but there should be no cases that demonstrate the outcome but not the condition.

This can be demonstrated using a simplified example, based on the analysis in this book. We want to work out the conditions that are necessary for the presence of high job search activity (henceforth referred to as H) amongst unemployed people across a range of European countries. We have identified certain conditions that we think might be a factor in determining high job search activity in the unemployment benefits that are paid to unemployed people. These are the degree of behavioural conditionality (C), the degree of universal coverage of unemployment benefits, measured by the ease of accessing unemployment benefits (U), and the marginal rates of tax experienced when moving from unemployment to employment on their employment income (T).

Using QCA we find that all the cases that are in the high job search activity set are also members of the high conditionality set. There are no countries that are in the high job search set, that are not also in the high conditionality set. Based on this analysis, we could say that countries that have high job search activity are a subset of the countries that have high levels of conditionality. We could therefore conclude that high levels of conditionality are necessary for the presence of high job search, which would essentially mean that high job search could not exist without the presence of conditionality.

The basic logic of sufficiency is that a condition can be considered sufficient for the presence of an outcome if, whenever the condition is present, the outcome is also present. In this sense, the condition is a subset of the outcome. Using the same example as for necessity, let us say that countries which are members of the high conditionality set are all members of the high job search set. For the test of sufficiency, there may be countries that are members of the high job search set, which are not members of the high conditionality set, but not countries who are members of the high conditionality set which are not members of the high job search set. This being the case we could conclude that the presence of high conditionality is sufficient for the presence of high job search. This is different from necessity, in that there may be other conditions that lead to the outcome aside from high conditionality. The sufficiency simply means that high conditionality alone is sufficient for the presence of the outcome. However, it may that sufficiency depends on a number of conditions combining, where the presence of multiple conditions existing in conjunction is required for the presence of an outcome. It is important to note that the statement that the condition is sufficient for the outcome generates expectations only about the value of the outcome for cases that exhibit the condition. Cases that are not members of the condition are not relevant for evaluating the sufficiency statement. They neither help confirm nor refute the claim, regardless of the membership score they may have in the outcome.

## How QCA Is Used in This Book

Two variations of QCA are used in this book. Firstly, fuzzy set ideal type analysis is used to identify the degrees to which each country shares the characteristics of basic income. It compares each welfare regime with the principles of basic income. Secondly, the book uses fuzzy set QCA to identify necessary and sufficient conditions for the presence of high and low levels of job search activity amongst unemployed people in each country. The QCA seeks to identify the impact of each basic income principle across a variety of contexts. Figure 4.1 demonstrates how QCA mediates between theory and empirical analysis when examining basic income.

It uses ideal type analysis to identify how to measure basic income mechanisms in existing welfare regimes against their ideal types set out in basic income definitions. It also enables empirical analysis to determine the degree to which they are a member of a set or not. It then engages in causal analysis, identifying necessary and sufficient conditions for the presence or absence of an outcome, in this instance the presence or absence of high job search intensity.

## Set Theoretic Foundations: QCA as a Framework for Studying Complex Social Policy

This chapter discussed Qualitative Comparative Analysis (QCA) as a methodological framework for studying social policy. QCA bridges theoretical concepts with empirical analysis through set theoretic techniques, using both fuzzy set ideal type analysis and fuzzy set QCA to examine complex causal relationships.

The methodology centres on several key concepts, including the creation of cases and sets and the process of calibration. QCA identifies necessary and sufficient conditions for outcomes, whilst addressing

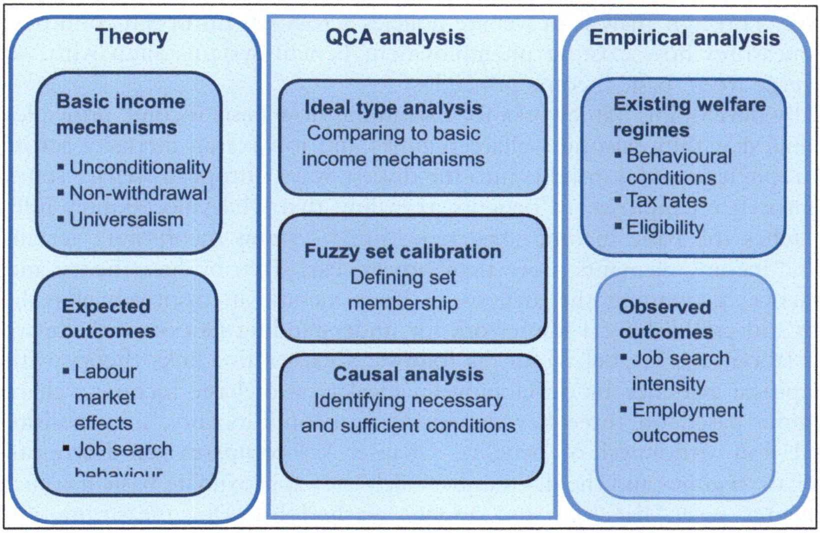


**Fig. 4.1** Using QCA to mediate theory and empirical analysis

unobserved combinations through counterfactual analysis. This approach recognises that social phenomena are subject to complex causation, where multiple paths can lead to the same outcome. The book applies QCA in two ways. Firstly, using fuzzy set ideal type analysis to measure how existing welfare systems compare to basic income principles. Secondly it uses fuzzy set QCA to identify necessary and sufficient conditions for job search behaviours.

The research focuses on specific cases, combining theoretical knowledge with empirical evidence through iterative analysis. This methodological approach enables careful examination of how basic income principles manifest in existing welfare systems and their effects on job search behaviour across European countries, enabling us to capture nuanced relationships between welfare policies and outcomes, whilst maintaining analytical rigour through systematic comparison and a clear theoretical grounding.

This leads us to Part Two of this book, which develops an ideal type basic income welfare regime based on three key dimensions: unconditionality, universalism (measured through accessibility), and participation tax rates. Through analysis of welfare policies across ten European countries, it measures how existing unemployment benefit systems align with, or diverge from, basic income principles.

By developing frameworks for examining how basic income principles manifest within existing welfare regimes and job search intensity across Europe, it provides insights into the diverse ways European welfare states approach unemployment benefits, revealing that whilst no country fully matches the basic income ideal type, some systems incorporate certain basic income elements more than others. Part Two bridges theory and practice, grounding the analysis of basic income in institutional realities and establishing a framework for understanding its potential impact on labour market behaviour, as follows: Chapter five links theory with empirical evidence by developing an ideal type of basic income welfare regime based on three key dimensions: unconditionality, universalism, and non-withdrawal of benefits. Chapter six compares ten European welfare regimes and the degrees to which they approximate basic income. Chapter seven develops and applies methodology for measuring job search intensity, based on time use data, which is then used in part three to examine how different welfare configurations influence behaviours.

## References


Befani, B. (2013). Between complexity and generalization: Addressing evaluation challenges with QCA. *Evaluation, 19*(3), 269–283. https://doi.org/10.1177/1474022213493839

Befani, B. (2016). Pathways to change: Evaluating development interventions with qualitative comparative analysis (QCA). Sztokholm: Expertgruppen för biståndsanalys (the Expert Group for Developent Analysis). Pobrane z: http://eba.se/en/pathways-to-change-evaluating-development-interventions-with-qualitative-comparative-analysis-qca [Preprint]. Retrieved April 21, 2025, from https://eba.se/wp-content/uploads/2016/07/QCA_BarbaraBefani-201605.pdf

Berg-Schlosser, D., et al. (2009). *Qualitative comparative analysis (QCA) as an approach*. Retrieved March 27, 2024, from https://dial.uclouvain.be/pr/boreal/object/boreal:81998

Blackman, T., Wistow, J., & Byrne, D. (2013). Using Qualitative comparative analysis to understand complex policy problems. *Evaluation, 19*(2), 126–140. https://doi.org/10.1177/1356389013484203

Blatter, J., & Blume, T. (2008). In search of co-variance, causal mechanisms or congruence? Towards a plural understanding of case studies. *Swiss Political Science Review, 14*(2), 315–356. https://doi.org/10.1002/j.1662-6370.2008.tb00105.x

Collier, D. (1998). Comparative method in the 1990s. *American Political Science Association-Comparative, 9*(1), 1–2.

Hanckel, B., et al. (2021). The use of qualitative comparative analysis (QCA) to address causality in complex systems: A systematic review of research on public health interventions. *BMC Public Health, 21*(1), 877. https://doi.org/10.1186/s12889-021-10926-2

Hudson, J., & Kühner, S. (2013). Beyond indices: The potential of fuzzy set ideal type analysis for cross-national analysis of policy outcomes. *Policy and Society, 32*(4), 303–317.

Kvist, J. (2007). Fuzzy set ideal type analysis. *Journal of Business Research, 60*(5), 474–481.

Mahoney, J. (2008). Toward a unified theory of causality. *Comparative Political Studies, 41*(4–5), 412–436. https://doi.org/10.1177/0010414007313115

Mahoney, J., & Goertz, G. (2006). A tale of two cultures: Contrasting quantitative and qualitative research. *Political Analysis, 14*(3), 227–249.

Markoff, J. (1990). A comparative method: Reflections on Charles Ragin's innovations in comparative analysis. *Historical Methods: A Journal of Quantitative and Interdisciplinary History, 23*(4), 177–181. https://doi.org/10.1080/01615440.1990.10594208

Oana, I.-E., Schneider, C. Q., & Thomann, E. (2021). *Qualitative comparative analysis using R: A beginner's guide*. Cambridge University Press. Retrieved March 14, 2024, from https://books.google.com/books?hl=en&lr=&id=lhA5EAAAQBAJ&oi=fnd&pg=PR7&dq=Qualitative+comparative+analysis+using+R&ots=G7YiEqyrWU&sig=VTMX64f07tPgGyjORIFl-3Qx9ig

Ragin, C. C. (1987). *The comparative method: Moving beyond qualitative and Quantitative Strategies*. University of California Press.

Ragin, C. C. (2000). *Fuzzy-set social science*. University of Chicago Press. Retrieved March 27, 2024, from https://books.google.com/books?hl=en&lr=&id=nZC2dLUH-OAC&oi=fnd&pg=PA1&dq=Ragin,+C.+(2000)+Fuzzy-set+social+science,+London:+The+University+of+Chicago+Press.+&ots=9QkG3Uuy0u&sig=1E2QvnU1NkHm1pkDb_ZP2Bgx6r8

Ragin, C. C. (2009a). *Redesigning social inquiry: Fuzzy sets and beyond*. University of Chicago Press. Retrieved March 14, 2024, from https://books.google.com/books?hl=en&lr=&id=WUj9yT5zAiIC&oi=fnd&pg=PR5&dq=redesigning+social+inquiry&ots=WvGzQMRoQQ&sig=JqfGnYO-LgdkvcFDR6gfel5GYoY

Ragin, C. C. (2009b). *Redesigning social inquiry: Fuzzy sets and beyond*. University of Chicago Press. Retrieved April 3, 2025, from https://books.google.com/books?hl=en&lr=&id=WUj9yT5zAiIC&oi=fnd&pg=PR5&dq=ragin+set+theory&ots=WvJCSPToPO&sig=FGB7aMmtQyc2NPBAvIbhEbGrfXs
Ragin, C. C. (2009c). *Redesigning social inquiry: Fuzzy sets and beyond*. University of Chicago Press. Retrieved April 22, 2025, from https://books.google.com/books?hl=en&lr=&id=WUj9yT5zAiIC&oi=fnd&pg=PR5&dq=Redesigning+social+inquiry:+Fuzzy+sets+and+beyond.&ots=WvJEPOMnUX&sig=nFiWJw3jNtFh3hW991dLKUQsICw
Ragin, C. C. (2014). *The comparative method: Moving beyond qualitative and quantitative strategies*. Univ of California Press. Retrieved March 27, 2024, from https://books.google.com/books?hl=en&lr=&id=2akwDwAAQBAJ&oi=fnd&pg=PR7&dq=Ragin,+C.+C.+(1987).+The+comparative+method+:+moving+beyond+qualitative+and++quantitative+strategies.+Berkeley,+CA.+%3B+London:+University+of+California+Press&ots=vfS8Ik3Wu2&sig=G-THxGeOTr8vk173Ts7YtI7RzRI
Ragin, C. C., Strand, S. I., & Rubinson, C. (2008). User's guide to fuzzy-set/qualitative comparative analysis. *University of Arizona, 87*, 1–87.
Rihoux, B., & Ragin, C. C. (2008). *Configurational comparative methods: Qualitative comparative analysis (QCA) and related techniques*. Sage Publications. Retrieved January 27, 2024, from https://books.google.com/books?hl=en&lr=&id=PnI-DQAAQBAJ&oi=fnd&pg=PP1&dq=ragin+2008+qca&ots=ZMECJGJqHv&sig=-_qxfiCyiZpjzi0eZ8XGDehu_90
Romme, A. G. L. (1995). Boolean comparative analysis of qualitative data: A methodological note. *Quality & Quantity, 29*(3), 317–329. https://doi.org/10.1007/BF01101977
Schneider, C. Q., & Wagemann, C. (2012). *Set-theoretic methods for the social sciences: A guide to qualitative comparative analysis*. Cambridge University Press. Retrieved March 16, 2024, from https://books.google.com/books?hl=en&lr=&id=RFIhAwAAQBAJ&oi=fnd&pg=PP16&dq=set+theoretic+methods+for+the+social+sciences&ots=ywJ81c10ot&sig=Cd0N2Of9sZa2urXYSTQMoijnGgo
Verkuilen, J. (2005). Assigning membership in a fuzzy set analysis. *Sociological Methods & Research, 33*(4), 462–496. https://doi.org/10.1177/0049124105274498

# Part II

CHAPTER 5

# Three Worlds of Basic Income: Developing an Ideal Type Basic Income Welfare Regime

**Abstract** Chapter five begins with an introduction to the historical and theoretical roots of welfare regime analysis, discussing the development of ideal type welfare regimes. It then moves onto develop a basic income ideal type welfare regime, measuring three dimensions of basic income: unconditionality, universalism and non-withdrawal of benefits. It applies the measures to welfare benefits for unemployed people across ten European countries. The analysis reveals how empirical examples of welfare regimes align or diverge from the ideal type basic income model, enabling readers to see the diversity of welfare systems across Europe as they relate to unemployed people.

**Keywords** Ideal type framework · Welfare mechanisms · Conditionality measurement · Accessibility to benefits · Participation tax rates · Comparative analysis · Welfare configurations

Whilst experiments provide valuable insights, their temporary nature and limited scope constrain our ability to understand how basic income might function within existing welfare institutions. This chapter develops an alternative approach, examining how basic income principles manifest across existing welfare regimes. The analysis focuses on three key



S. Watkins, *Basic Income, Work Incentives and Job Search Behaviour*, Exploring the Basic Income Guarantee,
https://doi.org/10.1007/978-3-031-99197-4_5

mechanisms that define basic income: unconditionality, universalism and non-withdrawal of benefits. Unconditionality represents the absence of behavioural requirements and sanctions that typically characterise welfare regimes. Universalism contrasts with welfare regimes that restrict access based on contributions, categorical eligibility, or means-testing. Non-withdrawal addresses the "unemployment trap" where benefits are withdrawn when entering employment.

Whilst evidence exists for these mechanisms in isolation, understanding how they interact requires a more systematic approach. This chapter develops an ideal type basic income welfare regime, measuring each country's proximity to the ideal basic income through analysis of conditionality (behavioural requirements, monitoring, and sanctions), accessibility (ease of obtaining benefits), and participation tax rates (financial incentives when moving from unemployment to employment). The analysis reveals that no country fully embodies the basic income ideal type, though Norway, Spain, the UK, and Greece show varying degrees of alignment along different dimensions. By mapping these patterns, we gain valuable insights into how basic income principles might be integrated into existing welfare systems and their potential effects on labour market behaviour.

## Three Key Mechanisms of Basic Income

Basic income represents a radical departure from traditional welfare approaches, yet its core principles appear, to varying degrees, in existing systems. By examining these principles as they operate in practice, we can better understand their potential effects. The analysis focuses on three key mechanisms that define basic income and directly influence job search behaviour: unconditionality, universalism and non-withdrawal of benefits.

### *Unconditionality*

Welfare regimes use varying levels of conditionality to encourage job search (Watts & Fitzpatrick, 2018), but also as a means of separating between those perceived to be 'deserving' of benefits and those who are not (Oorschot, 2000). This performative element of conditionality is now a constant in political environments, which seek to differentiate between those who are deemed to be making the requisite efforts to find or stay in paid work and those who are not. For this reason, the absence of conditionality represents the most controversial aspect of basic income.

The economic rationale for extensive use of conditionality across welfare regimes is that it provides necessary motivation to look for work, in the form of behavioural conditions, such as minimum job search requirements combined with monitoring of behaviour and a financial incentive to fulfil behavioural conditions in the form of sanctions. As chapter two sets out, the empirical research on the effects of conditionality suggest that its presence may decrease initial periods of unemployment, as people either take on paid work or move out of the benefit system. However, there are concerns over the longer term effects with the potential for repeated periods of unemployment. The only basic income experiment that focused on unemployed people, the Finnish experiment, suggests conditional requirements may not be necessary for maintaining job search activity. Many participants voluntarily continued using employment services even when not required to do so, bringing into question the assertion that higher levels of behavioural conditions are necessary to incentivise the unemployed to get back into work.

### *Universalism*

In basic income literature, the term 'universalism' relates to the fact that it is paid to everyone within a specified political community. It denotes the absence of circumstantial requirements for eligibility beyond citizenship or residence in a community (Van Parijs & Vanderborght, 2017). Receipt of basic income is not dependent on the occurrence of a specific social risk, nor on membership of a particular group or identifiable financial need. This stands in contrast to existing welfare regimes, where access to benefits is dependent on a range of factors, including:

Social insurance contributions. Most unemployment insurance schemes require a minimum level of social insurance contributions, based on previous work record.

Categorical eligibility. Many benefits are targeted at a specific section of society, where a need has been identified for additional financial assistance. For example, child benefit payments to parents of young children, sickness and disability payments.

Means-testing. Eligibility and entitlement to many benefits is dependent on a test of the income and wealth of benefit recipients, and commonly other members of their household. Those with too high an income or level of wealth are not eligible. For those who are eligible, means-tested benefits are reduced as income from other sources increases up to a point where entitlement to benefits is reduced to zero.

Citizenship/residency requirements. Many benefits, such as social assistance schemes, commonly require recipients to be either citizens and/or resident in the country or state where they are paid.

The lack of strict eligibility requirements therefore separates basic income from the range of benefits currently paid out. In contrast, the concept of welfare universalism is complex and multidimensional, with a variety of meanings at different levels and across contexts (Stefánsson, 2012). A single, agreed upon, definition of universalism does not exist. Rather there are 'varieties of universalism' (Anttonen & Sipilä, 2014), each dependent on the frame of reference and context in which the term is used (Kildal & Kuhnle, 2007). Such variety relates to whether universalism is defined at the regime level or specific policy level; the different mechanisms used to measure universalism and the ideological assumptions that justify its use in relation to social policy.

Universalism is therefore the most difficult principle to measure empirically, due to the various definitions used across the basic income and welfare literatures. Compared to measures of conditionality and marginal tax rates, there is less existing research examining the relationship between universalism and labour market participation.

As the focus of this book is on unemployed people, the analysis uses a measure of accessibility to unemployment benefits as a proxy for basic income universalism. Whilst there is little empirical evidence on the effects of basic income universalism on job search behaviour and labour market participation more broadly, in theory, the provision of universal benefits might act as a disincentive to look for work, particularly where the payments cover basic needs.

### *Non-Withdrawal of Benefits*

Basic income is paid irrespective of status in society. Many existing benefits, specifically unemployment benefits, are withdrawn when moving into paid work, and other benefits are means-tested away as income from other sources increases, resulting in the 'unemployment trap' discussed in chapter one, which results in many people being little or no better off when taking on work.

The empirical evidence examined in chapter two from the Finnish experiment specifically analysed the impact of reducing marginal effective tax rates on moving from unemployment to employment and found no significant effect on the amount of time spent in work over the course of the experiment (Kangas et al., 2021)(Watts & Fitzpatrick, 2018). Evidence from both the Alaska Permanent Fund Jones and Marinescu (2022) and Cherokee dividends (Akee et al., 2010) also suggest that non-withdrawable payments don't significantly reduce work motivation. These findings raise questions about whether a relationship exists between marginal tax rates and work incentives, which are addressed in this book.

## Measurement Approach and Analytical Framework

Whilst there is evidence of the effects of these mechanisms in isolation, there is limited evidence on how they interact to produce outcomes. The ideal type framework enables systematic analysis of these configurations by examining how they combine in practice. The approach bridges theory and practice by grounding analysis in existing institutional contexts, enabling direct comparisons to be made across a range of welfare regimes, and identifying how basic income principles function in practice, providing a better indication of how a basic income might impact on labour market activity.

Table 5.1 identifies each basic income principle and how it is developed into a welfare regime mechanism, used to measure their proximity to the pertinent basic income principle. This analysis reveals both the diversity of current approaches to welfare provisions and their relationship to basic income principles. Each measure is multidimensional and therefore consists of a number of sub-measures which are used to assess the different elements that make up each measure. The following section develops the measure of each mechanism.

### Conditionality

The measure of conditionality used in this book is based on the three main behavioural mechanisms that underpin conditionality:

**Table 5.1** Basic income mechanism and measures used

| *Basic income principle* | *Welfare regime measure* |
|---|---|
| Conditionality | Conditionality – Unconditionality |
| Non-withdrawal and no means-testing | High participation tax rate – Low participation tax rate |
| Universalism | High Accessibility – Low Accessibility |

1. Behavioural requirements that determine access to, and continued receipt of, benefits;
2. Monitoring techniques used to check compliance with behavioural requirements, and
3. Sanctions for non-compliance with behavioural and monitoring requirements (Watts & Fitzpatrick, 2018).

The mechanisms interact and are interdependent as 'incentives' to drive job search activity and increase employment rates. The first element sets out the behavioural requirements that an individual is required to undertake, these behavioural requirements are then monitored to ensure compliance. If compliance is lacking, then sanctions may be imposed to re-incentivise compliance.

The measure of conditionality used in this book is based on specific rules and regulations set out in legislation, or related documents and relies on a range of qualitative and quantitative data, including MISSOC ('Mutual Information System on Social Protection'), OECD data and country specific data kindly provided by the authors of a previous measure of conditionality (Knotz & Nelson, 2013). The following section sets out how each mechanism is measured.

### *Behavioural Requirements*

Behavioural requirements stipulate the actions an individual is required to take to maintain eligibility and entitlement to benefits. They take the form of 'work availability' requirements, which themselves have two elements. Firstly, they define what constitutes suitable forms of employment, which claimants should search for and accept if offered. Secondly, they set out job search activity requirements, specifying the amount of time or number of applications an individual should make in a specific period.

'Suitable employment' is defined as work that the unemployed person could reasonably be expected to take on, within certain parameters (Knotz & Nelson, 2013). If the potential job falls outside of the parameters, it is not deemed to be suitable, and the individual is under no obligation to either search for or take on such work.

Parameters vary across countries, both in nature and degree, and these form the first measure of behavioural requirements. The ideal type analysis begins from the two diametrically opposed ideal types. The first is the basic income ideal type, which does not impose any kind of behavioural requirements. In terms of 'suitable employment' this would translate as an unemployed person being able to refuse to either search for or take on any and all kinds of work. The opposite of this would be 'complete' conditionality, which translates as the unemployed being required to search for and accept and any and all kinds of work.

The measure of conditionality is therefore based on the principle that the more broadly suitable employment is defined, the higher the effective levels of conditionality, as a broader definition includes a wider range of jobs that the unemployed must consider searching and applying for. A very narrow definition of suitable employment therefore entails lower levels of conditionality, enabling the unemployed to disregard more jobs as outside the scope of 'suitable employment'.

Definitions of suitable employment are themselves based on a variety of factors including the unemployed person's previous work experience and personal circumstances, as well as the nature of the work itself. Due to their complexity, such requirements can be difficult to compare across countries. To overcome this, the analysis is based on statutory rules common to all countries included in the analysis (Ministry of Finance, 1998; Hasselpflug, 2005; Immervoll & Knotz, 2018; Knotz & Nelson, 2013; Langenbucher, 2015; Venn, 2012).

The analysis in this book focuses on four main areas where there is scope to refuse to search for, or take on, specific jobs. These are:

1. Occupational mobility—the right to refuse work outside of an individual's previous work experience.
2. Geographical mobility—the right to refuse work based on its location.
3. Previous earnings—the right to refuse work that is paid below levels of previous earnings.

4. Caring responsibilities—the right to refuse work owing to caring responsibilities.

### *Occupational Mobility*

Occupational mobility measures the degree to which unemployed benefit recipients may refuse offers of work based on their previous work experience. The ability to refuse jobs outside of one's previous experience is usually time limited. For example, in the UK, there is a 'permitted period' of up to 13 weeks during which jobseekers are allowed to look only for work in their 'usual occupation'.[1] Scoring of occupational mobility is therefore based on the period of time during which this exemption applies. Scores range from the requirement to accept a job in any sector immediately to the ability to refuse jobs in other occupational sectors for an indefinite period. The higher the level of occupational mobility that is required, the higher the level of conditionality.

### *Geographical Mobility*

Geographical mobility has previously been measured based on the distance that unemployed people are expected to travel for the purposes of work (Hasselpflug, 2005; Immervoll & Knotz, 2018; Knotz & Nelson, 2013; Venn, 2012). Many countries define geographical mobility in terms of either physical distance (in kilometres/miles) or maximum commuting time (in hours), and these form the basis of measures included in this analysis. Taking previous measures as a guide, the research in this book treats a commute of more than four hours per day as the highest level of conditionality. The least conditional circumstance is where no requirement to commute exists, and the claimant is free to determine their own geographical radius for job searching.

### *Previous Earnings*

Claimants of unemployment benefits may be required to accept a job at a rate of pay that is lower than their previous employment. The lower

[1] https://www.legislation.gov.uk/nisr/2024/18/pdfs/nisrem_20240018_en_001.pdf.

the rate of pay that must be accepted, the higher the level of conditionality. This is an important factor in conditionality as it impacts on the financial security of the unemployed. If they are required to take on work that pays significantly less than their previous wage, this may have a substantial impact on their standard of living. It is also an important factor when considering how unemployed people consider suitable work. The concept of the 'reservation wage', which is the lowest level wage a person is willing to accept for a job, is important in determining job search activity (Krueger & Mueller, 2016), and restrictions on people's ability to exercise this discretion is an important part of conditionality. For example, an individual may consciously, or otherwise, set a minimum salary or hourly wage below which they would not normally accept an offer of employment. This may be related closely to their previous job, as their standard of living may be linked to this minimum, and taking on a job which pays below this level would negatively impact on this standard.

### *Caring Responsibilities*

Caring responsibilities are also included as significant factors in determining the degree of behavioural conditionality in each country. The degree to which an individual's familial and household circumstances may be taken into account when determining 'suitable employment' is an important indicator of the degree of conditionality imposed by a welfare regime.

### *Suitable Employment Scores*

Table 5.2 contains the scores for each element of suitable employment, scored from 0 (no conditionality) to 6 (high conditionality). The maximum score is 24. The average score is 14.50, higher than the midpoint score of 12, suggesting that across European countries rules are strict regarding the circumstances under which an unemployed benefit recipient can refuse a job offer and still retain eligibility for benefits.

### *Job Search Activity Requirements*

The second part of behavioural requirements is the stipulation of a minimum level of specified job search activity, commonly defined in terms of either the amount of time an unemployed person must spend in job

**Table 5.2** Suitable employment scores

| *Country* | *Occupational mobility* | *Geographical mobility* | *Previous earnings* | *Caring responsibilities* | *Total* |
|---|---|---|---|---|---|
| Austria | 4 | 3 | 5 | 0 | 12 |
| Belgium | 4 | 5 | 5 | 3 | 17 |
| Finland | 4 | 4 | 5 | 6 | 19 |
| France | 0 | 2 | 2 | 4 | 8 |
| Germany | 6 | 4 | 4 | 6 | 20 |
| Greece | 0 | 1 | 5 | 4 | 10 |
| Italy | 6 | 4 | 6 | 3 | 19 |
| Norway | 6 | 0 | 5 | 1 | 12 |
| Spain | 2 | 5 | 5 | 1 | 13 |
| UK | 4 | 4 | 4 | 3 | 15 |

search activities, or a minimum number of job applications they must make, within a specified period.

The basic income ideal type requires no job search activity being completely unconditional. Defining the antithesis, 'complete' conditionality, presents a greater challenge. Although one might theoretically expect unemployed individuals to dedicate all waking hours to seeking employment, such expectations are impractical. Instead, a more reasonable definition of complete conditionality would establish the equivalent of a full working week (typically 35–40 hours) as the required commitment to job search activities. This creates a spectrum between zero required activity (basic income) and full-time job search (complete conditionality), providing a practical framework for measuring and comparing job search requirements across different welfare regimes. The actual policies implemented in various countries can then be assessed based on where they fall along this continuum, allowing for nuanced analysis of conditional elements within welfare programmes.

In most cases, there is no specified minimum level of job search activity. Only two countries specify a minimum, Belgium, and the UK. In Belgium, the number of job search activities that must be completed is not specified by the law. The necessary quantity depends on a variety of factors, but the average is 5 searches each month (OECD.org,a). The UK has, by far, the most stringent regulations on job search activities, mandating that benefit claimants search for 35 hours a week, less any agreed time spent in 'work preparation activities', voluntary and paid work

**Table 5.3** Job search activities scores

| *Country* | *Number or time spent on actions* | *Score* |
|---|---|---|
| Austria | No minimum | 1 |
| Belgium | Average of 5 per month | 2 |
| Finland | No minimum | 1 |
| France | No minimum | 1 |
| Germany | No minimum | 1 |
| Greece | NA | 0 |
| Italy | NA | 0 |
| Norway | No minimum | 1 |
| Spain | No minimum | 1 |
| UK | 35 hours per week, or expected hours | 6 |

(CPAG, 2016). Table 5.3 contains the scores for job search activities, ranging from 0 to 6.

### *Overall Score for Behavioural Requirements*

The overall score of behavioural requirements is a combination of both suitable employment and job search activity. The overall score is determined using calibration techniques set out in chapter three, setting fuzzy set scores and then combining sets according to fuzzy set theory.

Suitable employment and Job search activities are given equal weighting to determine an overall behavioural requirements score.[2] The two scores are then added together to give an overall score between 0 and 12, with 12 being the highest level of conditionality (Table 5.4).

The UK has the highest behavioural requirements, with a score of 9.75 out of 12. The lowest scores are Greece (2.50) and France (3.00), with the remaining cases scoring between 4.00 and 6.25. The UK score is increased greatly by the strict job search criteria, making it stand out compared to the other cases. In most countries, the relatively high suitable employment score is tempered by the low job search score, reducing the overall behavioural requirements score. The exception to this is the UK, which has high scores in both.

[2] To weight them equally, the valid reasons scores are divided by 4 to make them the same scale as the job search measure (0–6).

**Table 5.4** Behavioural requirement scores

| *Country* | *Suitable employment* | *Job search* | *Behavioural requirements* |
|---|---|---|---|
| Austria | 3 | 1 | 4 |
| Belgium | 4.25 | 2 | 6.25 |
| Finland | 4.75 | 1 | 5.75 |
| France | 2 | 1 | 3 |
| Germany | 5 | 1 | 6 |
| Greece | 2.5 | 0 | 2.5 |
| Italy | 4.75 | 0 | 4.75 |
| Norway | 3 | 1 | 4 |
| Spain | 3.25 | 1 | 4.25 |
| UK | 3.75 | 6 | 9.75 |

### *Monitoring of Job Search Behaviour*

Monitoring of behaviour is an important element of overall conditionality, linking required behaviours with the punitive element of conditionality, in the form of sanctions (Watts & Fitzpatrick, 2018). Behaviours monitored can range from overt and clearly visible actions, such as showing up for an appointment, or demonstrating how many job applications have been submitted, to more ambiguous attitudinal or dispositional measures of engagement, such as commitment, performance, or improvement in different tasks (Watts & Fitzpatrick, 2018). How desired behaviours are transformed into clear criteria that can be successfully monitored is thus a crucial issue in the design and efficacy of welfare conditionality (Pellerano & Barca, 2016).

However, there are limitations to what can be used as a measure of monitoring for the purposes of creating a measure of conditionality. It would be very difficult, for example, to attempt to measure demonstrable attitudinal changes towards job search. The measure of monitoring therefore focuses on the administrative elements of the mechanism.

Monitoring the behaviour of benefit claimants takes different administrative forms. The main forms relate to the requirement to 'sign in' to confirm unemployment status, interviews with case workers to check and discuss the claimant's job search activities and individual contracts known as 'Individual action plans' or 're-integration contracts' ("IAP"). IAPs set out the rights of the claimant in terms of the benefits to be paid and support provided, as well as the responsibilities of the claimant to search for work and the evidence required to support the level of actions taken (Hofmann et al., 2016). They represent an important change in the relationship between claimant and welfare regime, denoting a more detailed, intrusive form of conditionality (Watts & Fitzpatrick, 2018). The implication of using IAPs is that social rights are negotiable and therefore the rights themselves, such as the right to unemployment benefits, have been weakened (Handler, 2003), increasing conditionality.

The analysis in this book combines three elements of monitoring to reach an overall monitoring score.

- 'Checking in' requirements, which is how often unemployed people are required to 'check in' at the employment office and re-confirm their unemployed status.
- Checking of job search activities, relates to the frequency of monitoring of demonstrable job search activities undertaken by the unemployed.
- The extent to which IAPs are used.

From an ideal type analysis perspective, the measures begin with the basic income principle of no conditionality, which would manifest as no monitoring of job search behaviour. As with behavioural requirements, defining complete conditionality is more complex, and is based on an analysis of existing monitoring functions across European countries.

Each element is given equal weighting in determining the overall monitoring score (Table 5.5), with a score of 0 to 5 assigned to each, with 5 being the highest level of monitoring. A score of 0 means that no monitoring was effectively being undertaken.

Two countries have very high levels of monitoring. UK scores a maximum 15, with Austria close by at 14. France also has a high score (10). The remaining cases score between 2 and 7. It is noticeable that the Southern European countries (Greece, Italy and Spain) all have low, or very low monitoring and evaluation scores. This is different from the behavioural requirements score, where no such pattern was evident.

### *Sanctions*

Sanctions represent the 'punitive' element of welfare conditionality, in the form of financial penalties for non-compliance (Fletcher & Wright, 2018),

**Table 5.5** Monitoring scores

| *Country* | *Check in* | *Monitoring* | *IAP* | *Total* |
|---|---|---|---|---|
| Austria | 5 | 4 | 5 | 14 |
| Belgium | 1 | 2 | 3 | 6 |
| Finland | 4 | 1 | 4 | 9 |
| France | 2 | 3 | 5 | 10 |
| Germany | 1 | 1 | 5 | 7 |
| Greece | 1 | 0 | 1 | 2 |
| Italy | 4 | 0 | 0 | 4 |
| Norway | 5 | 0 | 0 | 5 |
| Spain | 1 | 1 | 0 | 2 |
| UK | 5 | 5 | 5 | 15 |

i.e. the withdrawal of benefits (Adler, 2016). They may be imposed for a variety of reasons and vary in magnitude and duration (Wu et al., 2006). However, they usually take one of three forms:

1. Loss of a proportion of benefits for a specified period.
2. Loss of all benefits for a specified period.
3. Loss of eligibility for benefits for a specified or indefinite period (Grubb, 2001).

The potential for sanctions commonly relates to four scenarios:

1. 'Voluntary' unemployment. Where the claimant becomes unemployed by voluntarily leaving employment or through misconduct.
2. Refusal of 'reasonable' job offers.
3. Failure to attend meetings and/or failure to provide evidence of job search activities.

Scores are based on the number of weeks sanctions are applied for, with longer periods of sanctions denoting higher levels of conditionality. The potential level of sanctions imposed may vary according to the number of infractions committed. For example, in most countries, sanctions increase based on the number of times a person refuses a job. In the UK, the sanction imposed for the first job refusal is 13 weeks. It increases to 26 weeks

**Table 5.6** Sanctions scores

| *Country* | *Voluntary unemployment* | *Refusal of job offer* | *Failure to report job search activities* | *Failure to provide evidence* | *Average* |
|---|---|---|---|---|---|
| Austria | 4 | 6.67 | 35 | 6.67 | 13.08 |
| Belgium | 9 | 17.67 | 5 | 5 | 9.17 |
| Finland | 12.86 | 17.38 | 15.33 | 8 | 13.39 |
| France | 17.33 | 6.19 | 15.33 | 7.67 | 11.63 |
| Germany | 12 | 3.43 | 8 | 8 | 7.86 |
| Greece | 40 | 40 | 40 | 40 | 40 |
| Italy | 40 | 40 | 40 | 0 | 30 |
| Norway | 11.71 | 11.71 | 6.29 | 0 | 7.43 |
| Spain | 40 | 17.33 | 40 | 11.73 | 27.27 |
| UK | 19.14 | 19.14 | 7 | 7 | 13.07 |

for a second refusal and 156 weeks for any further refusals. In other countries, such as Austria, Belgium and Finland, repeated refusals lead to the loss of eligibility.

This research uses the number of weeks as the score, up to 26 weeks. Sanctions for periods in excess of 26 weeks are scored the same as 26 weeks. This qualitative cut off point is based on the sanctions data itself. 26 weeks is generally the longest sanctions are imposed for across the sanction data analysed. The scores for more than 26 weeks (30), temporary suspension (35) and permanent suspension (40) increase slightly, so the highest sanction score is 40 (Table 5.6).

Southern European countries have high sanction scores, in contrast to the monitoring and evaluation scores. Four Countries, Finland, Austria, UK and France have mid-level scores, between 11.63 and 13.39, and the remaining three Countries, Belgium, Germany and Norway have low scores, between 7.43 and 9.17.

### *Overall Measure of Conditionality*

The next step is to combine the elements of conditionality to establish an overall conditionality score for each country. This is achieved through the combining of sets, based on set theoretic measures. Before combining the sets, fuzzy set scores for each dimension need to be established, using the

**Table 5.7** Calibration cut off points for conditionality scores

| | *Fully out of the conditional set* | *Neither in nor out of the conditional set* | *Fully in the conditional set* |
|---|---|---|---|
| Behavioural requirements (0–12) | 0 | 4.5 | 10 |
| Monitoring (0–15) | 0 | 5.5 | 13 |
| Sanctions (0–40) | 0 | 11 | 14 |

process of calibration, establishing qualitative thresholds which differentiate members of a set from non-members of a set. Table 5.7 sets out the qualitative cut off points used.

For a case to be fully out of the conditional set, it must have no behavioural requirements. For a case to be fully out of the conditional set in each mechanism, it must therefore have a score of 0, denoting the absence of conditionality.

The scores for being fully in the conditional set, are based on reasonable points at which it is assumed that the cumulative behavioural requirement or monitoring are of no further significance. For both behavioural requirements and monitoring, the scores are almost the maximum scores possible. For sanctions, the cut off point is lower, relatively speaking, at 14 which is the point at which previous measures of sanctions have deemed there to be no qualitative difference between 14 weeks or more (Ministry of Finance, 1998; Hasselpflug, 2005; Venn, 2012; Knotz & Nelson, 2013).

Cut off points for determining set membership and non-membership are more difficult to determine, given the lack of existing theoretical or empirical evidence to rely on. Instead, this analysis uses cut off points around the mid-point scores for each of the mechanisms, with the exception of sanctions, which uses a much lower cut off point. This is based on the banding of sanctions score used in previous conditionality measures (Ministry of Finance, 1998; Hasselpflug, 2005; Venn, 2012; Knotz & Nelson, 2013). Table 5.8 shows the calibrated fuzzy set scores for each conditionality mechanism.

For a case to be fully out of the conditional set, it must have no behavioural requirements. For a case to be fully out of the conditional

**Table 5.8** Fuzzy set scores for conditionality mechanisms

| *Case* | *Behavioural requirements* | *Monitoring* | *Sanctions* |
|---|---|---|---|
| Austria | 0.44 | 1.00 | 0.54 |
| Belgium | 0.66 | 0.45 | 0.42 |
| Finland | 0.61 | 0.67 | 0.55 |
| France | 0.33 | 0.80 | 0.51 |
| Germany | 0.64 | 0.60 | 0.36 |
| Greece | 0.28 | 0.18 | 1.00 |
| Italy | 0.52 | 0.36 | 0.90 |
| Norway | 0.44 | 0.45 | 0.34 |
| Spain | 0.47 | 0.18 | 0.84 |
| UK | 0.98 | 1.00 | 0.54 |

set in each mechanism, they must therefore have a score of 0, denoting the absence of conditionality.

From the set membership scores for behavioural requirements, monitoring and sanctions, as depicted in Fig. 5.1, we can see that there are four degrees of conditionality, which help to identify the most and least conditional welfare regimes. Finland and the UK are members of all three sets, making them the most conditional welfare regimes included in the analysis.

Four countries are members of two out of the three sets. Germany combines behavioural requirements with monitoring but is not a member of the sanctions set. In contrast, Italy is a member of the behavioural requirements and sanctions sets but not monitoring. Austria and France are members of the monitoring and sanctions sets but not the behavioural requirement.

Three countries are members of only one set. Belgium is a member of the behavioural requirements set, whilst Greece and Spain are members of the sanctions set. Norway stands alone as the only country that is not a member of any conditional sets and therefore has the least conditional welfare regime amongst all the countries included in the analysis.

The final stage of determining the overall scores for conditionality is the process of combining the fuzzy set scores for each mechanism into a single conditionality score. When using a set theoretic approach, there are three ways to combine sets to arrive at an overall score for set membership (Schneider & Wagemann, 2012).

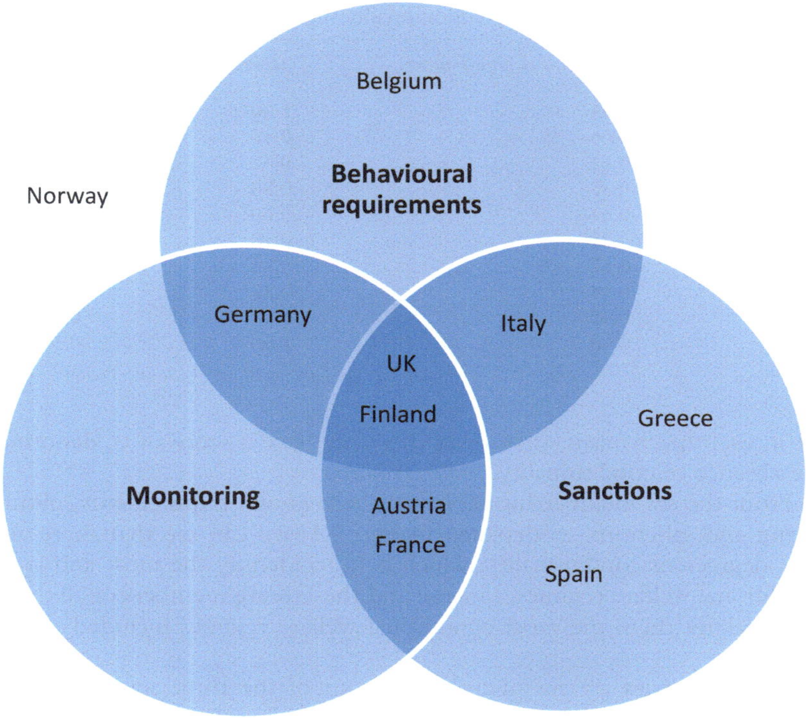


**Fig. 5.1** Venn diagram of conditionality set membership

1. The classical approach
2. Substitutability
3. Family resemblance

The classical approach requires that all secondary level conditions (i.e. behavioural requirements, monitoring and sanctions) must be present for the presence of the condition. Based on the classical approach, for high levels of conditionality to be present, all the secondary level conditions must be simultaneously present. If we use this method to combine the sets, only two countries would be in the conditional set, Finland and UK, whilst all other countries would be in the unconditional set. Membership of the conditional set means that a country is more conditional than unconditional, it does not have to be very highly conditional to be in the set. The requirement to be in each of the sub-sets to be a member of the overall conditional set therefore appears to be too stringent.

The second way to combine the set is the substitutability approach. Here, the presence of only one of the secondary level conditions would be necessary for the presence of high conditionality, so membership in any of the three secondary level conditions, behavioural requirements, monitoring or sanctions would be sufficient for the presence of conditionality. If we used this approach, all but one country, Norway, would be in the conditional set. All remaining countries would then be in the unconditional set. In contrast to the classical approach, this approach does not capture the range of conditionality across welfare regimes.

The third way of combining sets is the family resemblance approach, which requires the presence of any two secondary level conditions as sufficient for membership of the conditional set. A country that combines behavioural requirements with monitoring would be sufficient for membership of the conditionality set, as would a country that combined monitoring with sanctions or one that combined behavioural requirements with sanctions. Using this approach allows a broader number of countries to be included in the conditional set, whilst excluding those that are members of one or fewer of the secondary level conditions. This makes logical sense, in that countries which are members of two or three of the secondary level conditions are 'more' conditional than unconditional, whilst those who are members of one or fewer are 'more' unconditional than conditional. The family resemblance approach is therefore used to measure the overall conditionality of countries in this book.

### *Conditional and Unconditional Welfare Regimes*

Based on the family resemblance approach, six of the ten countries are in the conditional set. This is the qualitative measure of QCA, which separates those that are in the set, from those that are not. As Table 5.9 shows, the countries in the conditional set are Austria, Finland, France, Germany, Italy and UK. The countries in the unconditional set are Belgium, Greece, Norway and Spain.

Fuzzy set ideal type analysis enables not just qualitative, but quantitative analysis, highlighting not just which countries are in which membership set, but also the degree to which they are members of each

**Table 5.9** Fuzzy set scores for Conditionality

| *Set membership* | *Country* | *Conditionality score* |
|---|---|---|
| Conditional | UK | 0.98 |
| | Finland | 0.61 |
| | Germany | 0.6 |
| | Austria | 0.54 |
| | Italy | 0.52 |
| | France | 0.51 |
| Unconditional | Spain | 0.47 |
| | Belgium | 0.45 |
| | Norway | 0.44 |
| | Greece | 0.28 |

set. As Table 5.9 also demonstrates, the degree of set membership varies across welfare regimes in European countries.

The UK is the most conditional with a very set score of 0.98. The five other cases in the conditional set have lower scores. Finland and Germany have very similar scores (0.61 and 0.60 respectively), denoting relatively strong set membership. However, the remaining three countries in the conditional set have scores between 0.51 and 0.54, signifying that they are close to the qualitative cut off point between conditional and unconditional. This is particularly the case for France, with a score of 0.51, it is only just in the conditional set.

On the other side of the qualitative cut off point is Spain with a score of 0.47, only just in the unconditional set, along with Belgium with a score of 0.45 and Norway, 0.44. The lowest conditionality score is 0.28 for Greece, placing it strongly in the unconditional set. The next section undertakes the same process for establishing the measurement of accessibility.

## Accessibility

A central tenet of basic income is that it is universal, paid to everyone within a political community. The only eligibility requirement for a basic income in most literature is habitual residence in the political community, an inevitable corollary of formulating basic income as a 'citizenship' right (Puttick, 2020). For the purposes of this book, universalism is constructed as a measure of the ease of 'accessibility' to unemployment benefits.

Accessibility is measured in two specific ways. Firstly, a measure of the degree to which access to unemployment insurance benefits are dependent on periods of social insurance contributions linked to paid work or related activities. Secondly, a measure of the accessibility of social assistance schemes. The overall measure of Accessibility is then based on combining the Accessibility sets for unemployment insurance and unemployment/social assistance schemes.

Unemployment insurance and social assistance both provide financial support to unemployed individuals but differ in important ways. Unemployment insurance is paid individually regardless of household income and is not means-tested, but it does require previous work contributions, is generally paid out for defined periods, and is withdrawn when employment begins.

Social assistance is non-contributory, means-tested benefit, with flat rate payments for unlimited periods based on financial need. Generally, when an individual losses eligibility for unemployment insurance or is not eligible in the first place, they move onto social assistance. Some countries have a separate, specific unemployment assistance scheme, which functions in the same way as social assistance.

### *Accessibility to Unemployment Insurance*

All unemployment insurance schemes in the study specify a required record of paid employment for eligibility to unemployment insurance benefits. These requirements are most often expressed in terms of a combination of two factors.

Firstly, a minimum work record, based on a contributions period. This is measured by the number of weeks of contributions required for access to unemployment insurance benefits. Across the countries included in the book, this ranges from a low of 2 weeks contributions in Norway to a high of 78 weeks in Belgium. Three of the countries (Austria, Germany and Spain) require a year (52 weeks) of contributions, with all other countries setting requirements between 2 and 52 weeks.[3]

The second measure is called the 'reference period' and stipulates the period during which the minimum work record must be established. The reference period is, by necessity, either equal to or more than the

[3] Figures are based on those produced by MISSOC (Mutual Information System on Social Protection).

contributions period. For example, Austria requires 1 year (52 weeks) of contributions over the last 2 years (104 weeks). To gain access to unemployment insurance benefits in Austria, the unemployed individual must therefore have paid 52 weeks of contributions within the last two years prior to making the claim for benefits. The measure of Accessibility uses both to determine accessibility, together with a third, a ratio of contribution and reference periods.

The ratio relates the minimum work record to the reference period to provide an additional measure of accessibility. For this measure, higher ratio values indicate stricter qualifying conditions, and therefore lower accessibility scores. For example, Both Austria and Spain have a contribution period of 52 weeks. However, their reference periods are very different, giving different ratios. In Austria the ratio is 0.50 as it has a reference period of 104 weeks. Therefore, the contribution period is half the length of the reference period. However, in Spain the reference period is far longer, at 312 weeks, equivalent to six years. In Spain, the minimum contribution period can therefore be spread over a much longer period, which means that the Spanish unemployment insurance scheme is more accessible than the Austrian version, as it takes into account contributions for a far longer period. This is reflected in the ratio for Spain of 0.17. Table 5.10 contains the scores for each measure.

**Table 5.10** Social insurance contributions, weeks required for eligibility

| *Country* | *Contribution period* | *Reference period* | *Ratio* |
|---|---|---|---|
| Austria | 52 | 104 | 0.5 |
| Belgium | 78 | 116 | 0.67 |
| Finland | 34 | 104 | 0.33 |
| France | 17 | 120 | 0.14 |
| Germany | 52 | 104 | 0.5 |
| Greece | 29 | 104 | 0.28 |
| Italy | 52 | 104 | 0.5 |
| Norway | 2 | 52 | 0.04 |
| Spain | 52 | 312 | 0.17 |
| UK | 31 | 104 | 0.3 |

### *Accessibility to Social Assistance*

Eligibility for social assistance schemes is measured by a range of criteria. Unlike social insurance schemes, which are designed to address specific social risks, social assistance schemes are residual in nature, designed to support those in financial need. They are more akin to basic income in the sense that they do not generally require any present or historical link to the labour market, and cash benefits are paid irrespective of specific 'social risks', aside from the risk of poverty, together with residency requirements. However, they tend to differ from basic income in important ways. Firstly, they are means-tested, so a financial need must be established for receipt. In this sense, they are more akin to a negative income tax than a basic income. They occasionally include a nationality requirement, in addition to residency. There also tend to be separate schemes for those who are employed and those who are not. No such differentiation is made by basic income, which is a single scheme paid to all. The presence of multiple schemes opens up the potential for gaps into which people fall, and also administrative difficulties, particularly where people move between employment and unemployment on a regular, or indeed irregular, basis. Finally, there are differences in the legal rights to social assistance across European welfare regimes, which differentiate them from basic income, which is paid as a legal right, with no administrative discretion.

The research therefore uses four dimensions to measure the strictness of eligibility conditions for assistance schemes:

- Nationality
- Residence
- Categorisation
- Legal right/discretionary

Nationality measures whether cash benefits are limited to nationals of the particular country. Where nationality conditions exist, eligibility is deemed to be stricter. The residence test examines whether all residents are eligible or whether there are restrictions in terms of minimum period of residence. Categorisation measures the degree to which social assistance is provided in the form of a single scheme covering the whole working-age population or by multiple categorical schemes designed for different parts of the population. Basic income is a single scheme covering

**Table 5.11** Unemployment/social assistance Accessibility scores

| *Country* | *Nationality* | *Residence* | *Categorisation* | *Total* |
|---|---|---|---|---|
| Austria | 3 | 3 | 2 | 8 |
| Belgium | 2 | 3 | 2 | 7 |
| Finland | 4 | 3 | 4 | 11 |
| France | 4 | 3 | 2 | 9 |
| Germany | 2 | 4 | 2 | 8 |
| Greece | 1 | 1 | 1 | 3 |
| Italy | 3 | 4 | 2 | 9 |
| Norway | 4 | 4 | 4 | 12 |
| Spain | 4 | 2 | 2 | 8 |
| UK | 4 | 4 | 2 | 10 |

the whole population, so has high levels of coverage, whereas categorical schemes are, by their very nature, exclusive defining those who are eligible and those who are not. The more, specific schemes that a country has, the lower the level of Accessibility, due to the increased likelihood of certain sections of society falling into the gaps between schemes. Finally, the measure of legal right/discretion assesses the degree to which accessibility to social assistance is based on a well defined legal right or whether it is at the discretion of administrators. Table 5.11 shows the scores for each dimension.

*Calibration*

Accessibility to unemployment insurance is calibrated using three measures. For contribution periods, full accessibility requires zero contributions, whilst cases requiring over 102 weeks (2 years) are classed as completely inaccessible. The threshold between accessible and inaccessible is set at just less than a year, at 51 weeks. For reference periods (timeframe for making contributions), the fully inaccessible threshold is 26 weeks, the accessible/inaccessible boundary is 102 weeks, and full accessibility requires 204 weeks or more. The ratio score (contribution period divided by reference period) uses 1 as fully inaccessible (equal periods), 0.49 as the accessibility threshold, and 0 as fully accessible (no requirements). The overall accessibility score uses the 'family resemblance' method, requiring high scores in at least two of the three indicators.

Social assistance accessibility is based on cumulative scores across three indicators. Fully inaccessible schemes score 3 points (regional

**Table 5.12** Fuzzy set scores for unemployment insurance and social assistance

| *Country* | *Unemployment insurance* | *Social assistance* |
|---|---|---|
| Austria | 0.49 | 0.45 |
| Belgium | 0.32 | 0.36 |
| Finland | 0.66 | 0.86 |
| France | 0.83 | 0.57 |
| Germany | 0.49 | 0.45 |
| Greece | 0.71 | 0.00 |
| Italy | 0.49 | 0.57 |
| Norway | 0.96 | 1.00 |
| Spain | 0.83 | 0.45 |
| UK | 0.69 | 0.71 |

schemes restricted to nationals), whilst fully accessible schemes score 12 points (single nationwide scheme available to all working-age people with minimal residency requirements and no nationality restrictions). The threshold for accessibility is set at 8.5, requiring high scores (3 + ) in at least two indicators. The fuzzy set scores for each secondary level measure are shown in Table 5.12.

The venn diagram (Fig. 5.2) demonstrates the set membership of each secondary level measure.

From the set membership scores for unemployment insurance and social assistance, we can see that there are four countries which are members of both sets, Finland, France, Norway and the UK are members, making them the most accessible welfare regimes included in the analysis.

The three southern European countries are each member of a single set, Greece and Spain in the unemployment insurance and Italy in the social assistance sets. This leaves three countries outside of both sets, Austria, Belgium and Germany.

*Calculating the Overall Accessibility Fuzzy Set Score*

The final stage of determining the overall scores for conditionality is the process of combining the fuzzy set scores for each mechanism into a single conditionality score. When using a set theoretic approach, there are three ways to combine sets to arrive at an overall score for set membership.

The overall fuzzy set score for Accessibility is derived using the 'classical method', whereby all secondary level indicators must be present simultaneously for a case to be in the accessible set (Table 5.13). This is due to the fact that we do not know whether the unemployed measured in

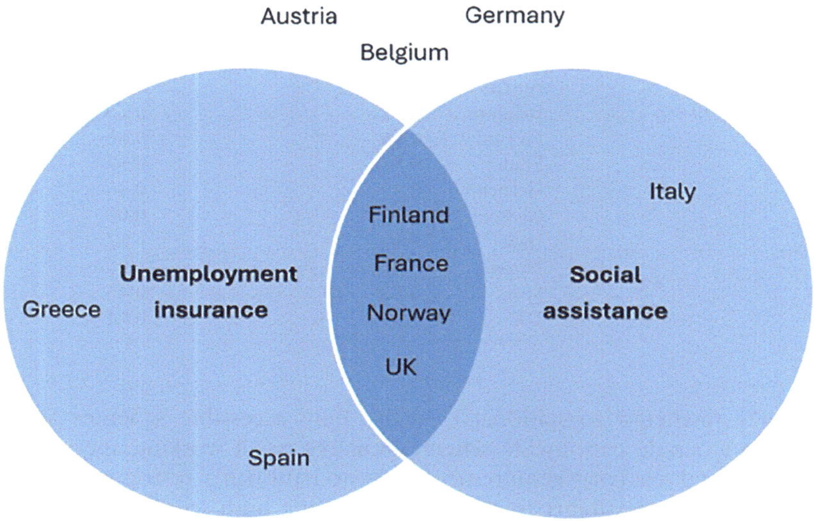


**Fig. 5.2** Venn diagram of accessibility set membership

the outcome are recipients of unemployment insurance or social assistance benefits, or indeed neither. The analysis therefore uses the most conservative approach to determining Accessibility.

Based on this approach, four cases are in the accessible set. Norway, is almost fully in (0.96), and UK (0.69), Finland (0.66) and France (0.57) are more in the set than out. Of the cases that are not in the accessible

**Table 5.13** Accessibility fuzzy set scores

| *Set membership* | *Country* | *Accessibility score* |
|---|---|---|
| Accessible | Norway | 0.96 |
| | UK | 0.69 |
| | Finland | 0.66 |
| | France | 0.57 |
| Inaccessible | Italy | 0.49 |
| | Austria | 0.45 |
| | Germany | 0.45 |
| | Spain | 0.45 |
| | Belgium | 0.32 |
| | Greece | 0.00 |

set, the three southern countries have split memberships, with Greece and Spain both being in the insurance accessible set, but not the assistance set. Austria, Belgium and Germany are in neither set for Accessibility.

The next section examines the measure of participation tax rates.

## Participation Tax Rates

As basic income is characterised by low marginal tax rates on moving from unemployment into employment, as it is neither withdrawn, nor means-tested away. Existing unemployment benefits are withdrawn when an individual ceases to be unemployed. Where this happens, significant financial disincentives can be created, whereby the individual may be little or no better off financially when moving from unemployment into work, as the net income received from employment may not exceed the net income from unemployment benefits. This disincentive has been characterised as an 'unemployment trap', which highlights the combined effects of benefit withdrawal, means-testing and the imposition of tax and social insurance contributions on paid work, that may result in low financial incentives to work.

The measure included in this book reflects the degree of financial disincentives built into the existing welfare regimes in each country. The measure calculates participation tax rates (PTR) for a range of household types to measure the financial disincentives of the unemployed seeking to move back into paid work.

The measure of PTR is a ratio of net income when unemployed and when employed. PTRs are measured as a percentage of the effective tax rate on income moving from unemployment to employment. The higher the PTR, the lower the net income difference between unemployment and employment, and therefore the higher the financial disincentive to move from unemployment into employment.

The measure of participation tax rates is formed of three secondary level measures. Two are measures relating to unemployment insurance, and a third based on social assistance. The measure of PTRs is based on the OECD TaxBen model, which calculate net incomes based on a range of factors, including work status, wage rates, hours worked and household characteristics to determine benefits and net wage income for a range of 'typical' households.

Participation rates tend to change depending on the length of the period of unemployment. This is usually a function of the expiration of unemployment insurance benefits, which are commonly based on levels of previous earnings and therefore more generous than unemployment or social assistance schemes, which pay a flat rate benefit. PTRs therefore tend to fall over time, as benefits become less generous, and the difference between unemployment income and earned income decreases.

For example, in Germany, there is a sharp decline in PTRs after 12 months of unemployment. Figure 5.3 shows the average PTRs for four household types between 2 and 60 months of unemployment. From an overall average of between 59 and 73% at 12 months to an average of 21% to 30% at 36 months.

Financial disincentives to work therefore vary over time. To reflect this, the calculation of average PTRs for unemployment insurance is split into two, based on 'short term' unemployment and 'long term' unemployment. The cut off point for 'long term' unemployment is 12 months. This is the definition of 'long term' unemployment used by the OECD (OECD.org,b). PTRs for social assistance recipients (those who did not qualify for unemployment insurance) are also calculated. Table 5.14 shows the participation tax rates scores for each country.

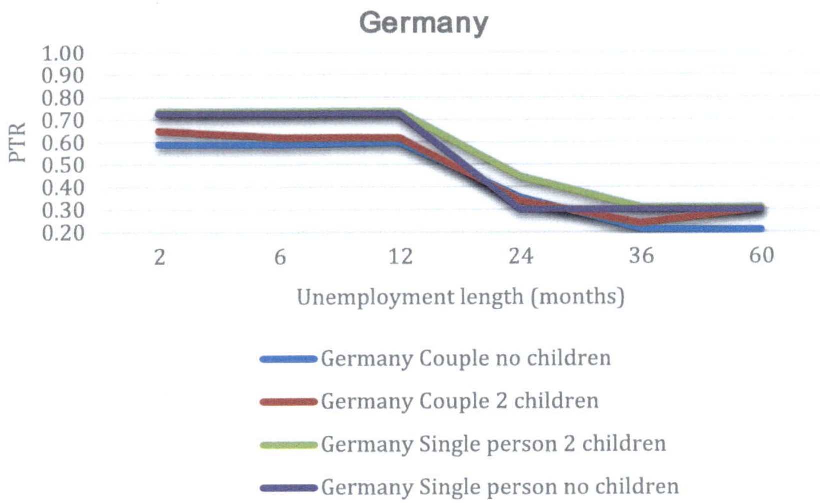


**Fig. 5.3** Participation tax rates in Germany between 0 and 60 months of unemployment

**Table 5.14** Participation tax rate scores

| *Country* | *Short Term PTR* | *Long Term PTR* | *Social assistance PTR* |
|---|---|---|---|
| Austria | 0.75 | 0.67 | 0.57 |
| Belgium | 0.74 | 0.67 | 0.59 |
| Finland | 0.73 | 0.62 | 0.59 |
| France | 0.81 | 0.62 | 0.48 |
| Germany | 0.68 | 0.38 | 0.63 |
| Greece | 0.62 | 0.28 | 0.24 |
| Italy | 0.74 | 0.53 | 0.14 |
| Norway | 0.65 | 0.49 | 0.63 |
| Spain | 0.53 | 0.48 | 0.41 |
| UK | 0.54 | 0.52 | 0.53 |

The cut off point being fully out of the High PTR set is 0.10, equivalent to an effective tax rate of 10% of earned income. This is deemed to be low enough as to not impact on the decision making of an individual. The cut off point for being fully in the high participation set is 0.90, equivalent to an effective tax rate of 90% of earned income. This is based on Rantala (1999), who defined the unemployment trap, where an unemployed worker is unable to increase the household's disposable income by more than 10% through employment. The cut off point for being in the high participation tax set is set at slightly above 0.50. The 0.50 point makes sense as a cut off point as it is the point at which more of an individual's income is lost in reduced benefits and increased taxes, than is retained by the individual. However, the cut off point is set slightly higher than 0.50 to account for the differences in PTRs across short term, long term, and social assistance PTRS, and is set at 0.56. The impact of which is to reduce the skew of cases in the high participation tax rate set if a calibration point of 0.50 is used.

From the set membership scores for short term, long term and social assistance depicted in Fig. 5.4, we can see that there are three countries in the high PTR set for all three secondary level measures, Austria, Belgium and Finland. Germany and Norway are both the short term and social assistance sets, whilst France is in the short term and long term sets. Italy and Greece are members of the short term set only, with the other Southern European country, Spain and the UK in none of the sets. It is interesting to note that eight out the ten countries are in the short term set, and no countries have high PTRs for social assistance or long term alone. This appears to be a function of unemployment insurance schemes, which produce high levels of financial disincentives over the short term. Once eligibility to unemployment insurance ceases, PTRs tend to fall. Only Spain and the UK are not in the short term set, owing largely to comparably low levels of benefits paid under their unemployment insurance schemes.

To combine the sets to get to an overall fuzzy set score for high participation tax rates, the family resemblance method is used, so that, for a case to be in the high participation tax rate set, at least two of the three secondary level indicators must be present. The overall scores for High PTR are in Table 5.15.

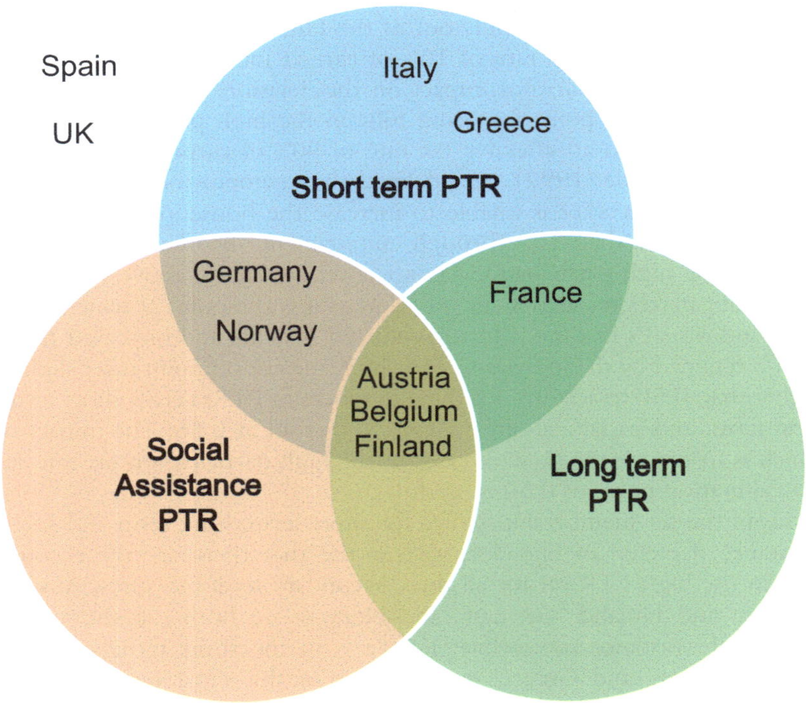


**Fig. 5.4** Venn diagram of PTR set membership

**Table 5.15** Fuzzy set scores for PTR

| *Set membership* | *Country* | *PTR* |
|---|---|---|
| High PTR | Austria | 0.66 |
| | Belgium | 0.66 |
| | Germany | 0.60 |
| | Norway | 0.60 |
| | Finland | 0.59 |
| | France | 0.59 |
| Low PTR | Italy | 0.47 |
| | UK | 0.47 |
| | Spain | 0.41 |
| | Greece | 0.20 |

There are six cases in the High PTR set, Austria, Belgium (both 0.66), Finland, France (both 0.59), Germany (0.60) and Norway (0.60). None of the cases have particularly high fuzzy set scores, due to the ranges of PTRs amongst short and long term and social assistance. Of the four cases in the low PTR set, Greece has the lowest score (0.20), with Italy, Spain and UK all in the 0.4 range.

## Basic Income Ideal Type Welfare Regime

The basic income ideal type welfare regime consists of the following three attributes; unconditional, accessible and low participation tax. As the venn diagram (Fig. 5.5) shows, there are no cases amongst those included in the analysis that are in the basic income ideal type set. This is not surprising given the nature of contemporary welfare regimes for the unemployed, and the desire to undertake basic income experiments across European countries. As the analysis of the cases has shown, most countries' welfare regimes for the unemployed are characterised by either high levels of conditionality, high levels of participation taxes or low Accessibility to unemployment benefits.

The closest to a basic income ideal type are Norway, Spain and UK, each of which are in two of the three sets. There are two countries which are completely out of the basic income sets, Austria and Germany are neighbours both geographically and in terms of set membership in the fuzzy ideal type welfare regimes. They combine high conditionality, low accessibility and high participation tax. These two can be said to be the least like a basic income. There is one country in the unconditional set,

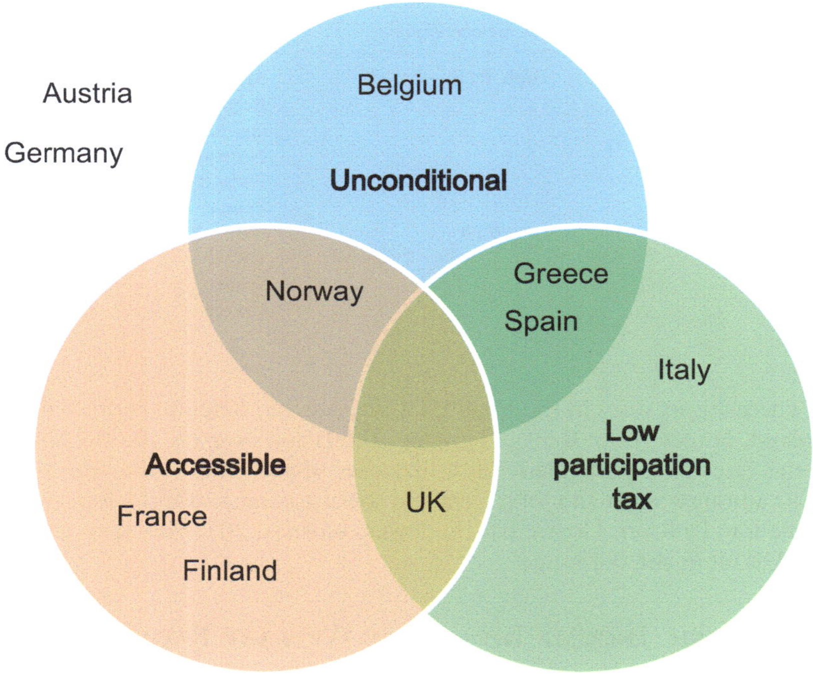


**Fig. 5.5** Basic income ideal type welfare regime set membership

but neither of the other sets, Belgium, has low conditionality, but also low accessibility and high participation tax. Italy has low participation tax rates, but high conditionality and low accessibility. Finland, rather surprisingly given the commonly made assumption it would be the most like a basic income is in the accessible set, but not the unconditional and low participation tax sets. This makes sense, from a conditionality perspective at least, given the conditional 'turn' in Finland in the years building up to 2010 (Duell, Grubb & Singh, 2009). High participation taxes also make sense for a country with generous and comprehensive benefits, based on previous earnings. France is in the same part of the Venn as Finland.

The three southern European countries Greece, Italy and Spain are all in the low participation tax set. This is largely because of the low benefits payable to recipients, reducing the impact of moving from benefits to paid work. However, Greece and Spain are also in the unconditional set, unlike Italy. They therefore share two out of the three elements of basic income—low participation tax and low conditionality. However, they are both in the low accessibility set.

The UK is also in two of the three sets, being both accessible and with low participation tax rates. However, the UK has the highest conditionality score of all the countries included in the analysis. This leaves Norway, which is perhaps the closest to a basic income, being in the unconditional set, as well as the accessible set. The only aspect which separates it from the basic income ideal type is its membership in the high participation tax set.

Norway is perhaps best described as the closest to as basic income ideal type from an ideological perspective, in that it has high levels of accessibility, and been described (along with Finland) as an example of a 'universal' welfare system and has low levels of behavioural conditionality.

## Principles to Mechanisms: Creating an Ideal Type Framework for Welfare Analysis

This chapter developed an ideal type basic income welfare regime and used it to measure the welfare regimes of ten European countries, as they relate to unemployed people claiming unemployment benefits. The analysis identified that none of the countries are in the basic income ideal type set, with four countries being in two out of the three sets. The closest to a basic income ideal type were Greece, Norway, Spain and the UK.

The absence of any country that fully embodies the basic income ideal type highlights the radical departure that basic income represents from existing welfare regimes. Even countries often assumed to be closer to basic income principles, such as Finland, diverge significantly in key areas. This finding demonstrates that basic income represents a distinct welfare paradigm rather than merely an extension or modification of existing approaches.

The ideal type framework developed in this chapter makes several important contributions to the study of basic income. Firstly, it provides a systematic method for measuring how closely existing welfare systems approximate basic income principles. This creates a foundation for understanding how different configurations of these principles might influence behaviour, particularly job search activity. By identifying which countries most closely resemble basic income along specific dimensions, the framework enables more nuanced predictions about how basic income might function across different institutional contexts.

Secondly, the analysis reveals important institutional patterns across European welfare regimes. Norway's combination of unconditionality and accessibility but high participation tax rates differs significantly from the UK's approach of high conditionality with accessibility and low participation tax rates. These contrasting welfare configurations provide natural laboratories for examining how basic income principles influence job search behaviour in different institutional contexts, which is explored in subsequent chapters.

Thirdly, the analysis identifies potential institutional pathways towards basic income implementation. The findings suggest that different welfare regimes may require distinct reform strategies based on which basic income principles they already approximate. For instance, Nordic countries might focus on reducing participation tax rates, whilst Southern European countries might prioritise improving accessibility.

This chapter also establishes the foundation for the empirical analysis in Part Three, where the relationship between welfare configurations and job search behaviour is examined. By mapping how basic income principles manifest in existing welfare systems, we can better understand their potential effects on behaviour when combined in the form of an actual basic income policy. The ideal type framework thus bridges theory and practice, grounding analysis in institutional realities whilst enabling systematic comparison across diverse welfare contexts. This approach addresses a key limitation in current basic income research by providing an empirical basis for understanding how basic income principles function in practice, moving beyond the speculative claims that often characterise basic income debates.

The next chapter builds on the findings from this one, examining how basic income principles manifest in existing welfare systems across Europe. Through a comparative analysis of ten European countries, Chapter 5 maps the degree to which each welfare regime approximates basic income mechanisms: unconditionality, universalism and non-withdrawal of benefits. The analysis reveals distinct institutional patterns and configurations that provide context for understanding their implications for job search behaviour. By identifying which welfare systems most closely approximate basic income ideals, the next chapter offers insights into the institutional pathways that might facilitate basic income implementation in different contexts.

## References


Adler, M. (2016). A new leviathan: Benefit sanctions in the twenty-first century. *Journal of Law and Society, 43*(2), 195–227. https://doi.org/10.1111/j.1467-6478.2016.00749.x

Anttonen, A., & Sipilä, J. (2014). Varieties of universalism. In *Draft paper prepared for the UNRISD Conference, New Directions in Social Policy: Alternatives from and for the Global South, Geneva* (pp. 7–8). Citeseer. Retrieved April 20, 2024, from https://citeseerx.ist.psu.edu/document?repid=rep1&type=pdf&doi=d533527e6d2d9a7ff5b36b403b5ffd20607f1871

Duell, N., Grubb, D., & Singh, S. (2009). *Activation policies in Finland*. Retrieved April 18, 2024, from https://www.oecd-ilibrary.org/content/paper/220568650308

Fletcher, D. R., & Wright, S. (2018). A hand up or a slap down? Criminalising benefit claimants in Britain via strategies of surveillance, sanctions and deterrence. *Critical Social Policy, 38*(2), 323–344. https://doi.org/10.1177/0261018317726622

Grubb, D. (2001). Eligibility criteria for unemployment benefits. *Labour Market Policies and Public Employment Service* [Preprint]. Retrieved April 18, 2024, from https://books.google.com/books?hl=en&lr=&id=4ND0SKZv-5cC&oi=fnd&pg=PA187&dq=Grubb,+D.+(2000)+Eligibility+criteria+for+unemployment+benefits.+OECD+Economic+Studies,+31,+147-184.&ots=a_A_Z8MNSU&sig=S5PSRaxUO2WkU8iOXdujsrQ79es

Handler, J. F. (2003). Social citizenship and workfare in the US and Western Europe: From status to contract. *Journal of European Social Policy, 13*(3), 229–243. https://doi.org/10.1177/09589287030133002

Hasselpflug, S. (2005). Availability criteria in 25 countries. *Finansmi*. Retrieved April 18, 2024, from https://en.fm.dk/media/25936/working-paper-122005.pdf

Hofmann, B., et al. (2016). Do mandatory integration contracts improve job search outcomes of the unemployed? Evidence from a randomized controlled experiment in Germany. In *VfS annual conference 2016 (Augsburg): Demographic change*. Verein für Socialpolitik/German Economic Association. Retrieved April 18, 2024, from https://ideas.repec.org/p/zbw/vfsc16/145757.html

Immervoll, H., & Knotz, C. (2018). *How demanding are activation requirements for jobseekers?* Retrieved April 18, 2024, from https://papers.ssrn.com/sol3/papers.cfm?abstract_id=3234227

Jones, D., & Marinescu, I. (2022). The labor market impacts of universal and permanent cash transfers: Evidence from the Alaska Permanent Fund. *American Economic Journal: Economic Policy, 14*(2), 315–340.

Kangas, O., et al. (2021) *Experimenting with unconditional basic income: Lessons from the Finnish BI experiment 2017–2018*. Edward Elgar Publishing. Retrieved February 7, 2024, from https://books.google.com/books?hl=en&lr=&id=d3g8EAAAQBAJ&oi=fnd&pg=PR1&dq=Experimenting+with+Unconditional+Basic+Income:+Lessons+from+the+Finnish+BI+...&ots=TOiHW1qqm5&sig=V_cSv1zIVC4jCNSNQxqho7yx8vQ

Kildal, N., & Kuhnle, S. (2007) *Normative foundations of the welfare state: The Nordic experience*. Routledge. Retrieved April 20, 2024, from https://books.google.com/books?hl=en&lr=&id=HFEX-6VzpGEC&oi=fnd&pg=PR1&dq=Normative+foundations+of+the+welfare+state:+the+Nordic+experience.&ots=DtywjjCx84&sig=KLMBG82Lqm3_auRINwqzPnB4lls

Knotz, C., & Nelson, M. (2013). Quantifying 'conditionality': A new database on conditions and sanctions for unemployment benefit claimants. *Available at SSRN 2328253* [Preprint]. Retrieved April 18, 2024, from https://papers.ssrn.com/sol3/papers.cfm?abstract_id=2328253

Krueger, A. B., & Mueller, A. I. (2016). A contribution to the empirics of reservation wages. *American Economic Journal: Economic Policy, 8*(1), 142–179.

van Oorschot, W. (2000). Who should get what, and why? On deservingness criteria and the conditionality of solidarity among the public. *Policy & Politics, 28*(1), 33–48.

Pellerano, L., & Barca, V. (2016) *The conditions for conditionality in cash transfers*. Retrieved April 18, 2024, from https://ipcig.org/pub/eng/OP317_The_conditions_for_conditionality_in_cash_transfers.pdf

Puttick, K. (2020). A UK 'Basic Income'? Testing the limits of universality. *Journal of Social Security Law*, 27(2). Retrieved April 22, 2025, from https://papers.ssrn.com/sol3/papers.cfm?abstract_id=3578427

Rantala, J. (1999). Household economic incentives, the unemployment trap and the probability of finding a job. *International Tax and Public Finance, 6*, 361–378.

Schneider, C. Q., & Wagemann, C. (2012) *Set-theoretic methods for the social sciences: A guide to qualitative comparative analysis*. Cambridge University Press. Retrieved March 16, 2024, from https://books.google.com/books?hl=en&lr=&id=RFIhAwAAQBAJ&oi=fnd&pg=PP16&dq=set+theoretic+methods+for+the+social+sciences&ots=ywJ81c10ot&sig=Cd0N2Of9sZa2urXYSTQMoijnGgo

Stefánsson, K. (2012). What is in a word? Universalism, ideology and practice. In *Welfare state, universalism and diversity* (pp. 42–68).

Van Parijs, P., & Vanderborght, Y. (2017). Basic income: A radical proposal for a free society and a sane economy. *Harvard University Press*. https://doi.org/10.4159/9780674978072

Venn, D. (2012). Eligibility criteria for unemployment benefits: Quantitative indicators for OECD and EU countries. Retrieved April 18, 2024, from https://www.oecd-ilibrary.org/content/paper/5k9h43kgkvr4-en

Watts, B., & Fitzpatrick, S. (2018) *Welfare conditionality*. Routledge. Retrieved March 30, 2024, from https://www.taylorfrancis.com/books/mono/10.4324/9781315652047/welfare-conditionality-beth-watts-suzanne-fitzpatrick

Wu, C.-F., et al. (2006). How do welfare sanctions work? *Social Work Research, 30*(1), 33–50.

CHAPTER 6

# Comparing Welfare Regimes to Basic Income Ideals

**Abstract** Chapter six examines the degree to which basic income principles exist across ten European welfare regimes. It analyses unemployment benefits across European countries through the lens of unconditionality, accessibility, and participation tax rates to identify distinct institutional patterns amongst welfare regimes that provide context for understanding their impact on job search behaviour, which is examined in subsequent chapters. The chapter reveals which welfare configurations most closely approximate basic income, which represent its antithesis, and the institutional pathways that might facilitate basic income implementation in different contexts.

**Keywords** Welfare regime clusters · Basic income ideal type welfare regime · Welfare typologies · Institutional patterns · Work incentives · Job search expectations · Comparative institutional analysis

The previous chapter developed an ideal type framework for measuring three key basic income mechanisms, unconditionality, universalism, and non-withdrawal of benefits, and universalism in existing welfare regimes. This chapter maps each country's set membership in relation to basic income, using fuzzy set ideal type analysis. This approach enables



S. Watkins, *Basic Income, Work Incentives and Job Search Behaviour*, Exploring the Basic Income Guarantee,
https://doi.org/10.1007/978-3-031-99197-4_6

researchers to identify qualitative differences between welfare regimes and measures the degree to which each approximates basic income. The comparative analysis serves multiple purposes. At a theoretical level, it reveals how basic income mechanisms manifest in existing welfare regimes. Most importantly for this book's focus, it provides context for understanding how these mechanisms influence job search behaviour. The chapter proceeds in three stages. Firstly, it examines each mechanism in isolation. It then analyses configurations of mechanisms across countries and finally assesses their combined effects on job search incentives. This three-stage analytical approach is particularly relevant in this context because it allows us to disentangle the complex relationships between welfare mechanisms that are often conflated in basic income debates. By first examining each mechanism independently, it is possible to identify their distinct characteristics across welfare regimes before analysing how they interact in configuration. This methodological progression connects to the broader argument by demonstrating that basic income's potential effects cannot be understood by considering its principles in isolation, as is often done in theoretical debates. These principles function as part of complex institutional ecosystems where outcomes emerge from the interaction of multiple mechanisms. This systematic examination provides a foundation for the subsequent analysis of job search behaviour in Chapter Six, allowing us to assess whether welfare regimes that more closely approximate basic income produce distinct patterns of labour market engagement compared to those that diverge from its core principles.

## Mapping Basic Income Ideal Type Mechanisms

This section examines each basic income principle in isolation before looking at them in combination, examining welfare configurations and basic income ideal types of welfare regimes.

### *Unconditionality*

As discussed in chapter four, the measure of unconditionality is based on three secondary level mechanisms which combine to create conditionality, behavioural requirements, monitoring, and sanctions. Using fuzzy set ideal type methodology enables researchers to identify qualitative differences in terms of overall set memberships, identifying ideal types. It also allows measurement of the degree to which each country represents a member of both the unconditional and conditional sets. Set membership scores vary significantly across the countries examined, revealing some distinct patterns.

Four countries fall into the unconditional set: Greece (0.72), Norway (0.56), Belgium (0.55), and Spain (0.53). Whilst Greece has the overall highest unconditional score, making it a strong member of the unconditional set, Norway demonstrates the most consistent unconditionality across all three secondary level measures, scoring above the qualitative cut off point (0.50) for membership in all three (behavioural requirements, monitoring, and sanctions). Both Greece's and Spain's path to the unconditional set is a somewhat unexpected combination of low levels of behavioural requirements and monitoring combined but with stringent sanctions. Belgium has a different configuration of secondary level memberships leading to membership of the unconditional set, combining high behavioural requirements, but low monitoring and sanctions. These patterns reveal that unconditionality manifests differently across welfare systems. In Norway, it suggests a deliberate policy approach emphasising autonomy, or what Haagh (2011) refers to as the 'complementarities', which are likely to increase control over time and therefore have a freedom enhancing effect on behaviour. Whilst in the Southern European countries of Greece and Spain, as well as Belgium, unconditionality may result more from limited institutional capacity for enforcement than from intentional policy design.

The remaining six countries are in the conditional set: the UK (0.98), Finland (0.61), Germany (0.60), Austria (0.54), Italy (0.52), and France (0.51). The UK stands out with a near maximum conditionality score, reflecting its extensive behavioural requirements, intensive monitoring, and stringent sanctions. This represents the furthest departure from basic income's unconditional principle. Other countries are far less conditional in their approach but remain in the conditional set. Both Italy and France have conditionality scores very close to the cut off point for set membership and are therefore in the area of most uncertainty, combining elements of conditionality and unconditionality almost equally. Both Finland and the UK are members of every secondary level measure, combining high behavioural requirements with strict monitoring and stringent sanctions. It is interesting to note the divergent paths of the two Nordic countries included in the analysis, as in contrast to Finland, Norway is a member of none of the secondary level conditional sets, making it the least conditional country in this respect. Austria and France combine high monitoring with, stringent sanctions, but low levels of behavioural requirements, displaying characteristics of both unconditionality and conditionality. However, both are within the overall conditional set, with strong administrative requirements to demonstrate job search activities, supported by the strong threat of sanctions. Germany and Italy have differing approaches to conditionality. Both are in the overall conditional set, but whilst Germany combines high behavioural requirements with strict monitoring but lax sanctions, Italy combines high behavioural requirements with stringent sanctions but lax monitoring.

The divergence of routes to conditionality suggests important differences in the approach to conditionality across countries. Finland and the UK appear to have a strong belief in the benefits of conditionality, whereas the other countries fall into the conditional set by reason of combining two out of the three conditionality measures, suggesting a less focused approach to conditionality and its enforcement.

### *Accessibility*

Accessibility, which acts as a proxy for the basic income principle of universalism, is defined by the ease with which individuals can access unemployment benefits, irrespective of work history or categorical restrictions, and also demonstrates significant variation amongst the countries included in the analysis. Four countries are in the accessible set: Norway (0.96), the UK (0.69), Finland (0.66), and France (0.57). Norway stands out with a near maximum score, combining relatively easily accessible unemployment insurance benefits, with a universal, non-categorical social assistance scheme. This is the closest approximation to the universalism of basic income amongst all of the countries included in the analysis.

The analysis reveals two distinct approaches to accessibility. The Nordic model, exemplified by Norway and, to a lesser extent Finland, emphasises universal coverage through complementary insurance and assistance schemes (Anttonen, 2012; Kildal & Kuhnle, 2007). In contrast, the UK system achieves accessibility through categorical, but broadly accessible assistance schemes that supplement a limited insurance scheme. The main difference between insurance and assistance schemes in the UK is the lack of means-testing of the insurance scheme.

There are six countries in the inaccessible set. Whilst Greece has the highest inaccessibility score (1.00), meaning that it is a full member of the inaccessible set, it actually has a low inaccessibility score for unemployment insurance. This means that Greece combines a relatively accessible unemployment insurance scheme with a very inaccessible social assistance scheme, creating large gaps through which may unemployed people fall, leaving them without financial safety net. Finally, Austria, Belgium, and Germany are all non-members of both secondary level measure sets of accessibility, making them the least accessible.

### *Participation Tax Rates*

Participation tax rates are a measure of the financial incentive or disincentive to move from unemployment into paid work (Torry, 2013; Martinelli, 2017). They measure the marginal effective tax rates on additional income from paid work following the removal of unemployment benefits and reduction, through means-testing, of additional benefits. High participation tax rates create a financial disincentive to work and have been described as creating an 'unemployment trap', where people are no better off by moving into work (Adam, Brewer & Shephard, 2006). A basic income smooths the process, as it is not withdrawn, nor means-tested, resulting in lower participation tax rates, which have been attributed with incentivising qualities, as people get to keep more of their income from moving into work. Although the empirical evidence to support this theory is lacking.

Four countries are in the low participation tax rate set: Greece (0.80), Spain (0.59), Italy, and the UK (both 0.53). These lower rates primarily reflect less generous benefit levels, rather than a deliberate attempt to institute low participation tax rates, as a means of incentivising entry into paid work. Greece's high score in the set results from minimal benefit levels that effectively create little financial disincentive to work.

Six countries are in the high participation tax rate set, Austria and Belgium (both 0.66), Germany and Norway (both 0.60), and Finland and France (both 0.59). These high rates generally correspond with more generous benefit levels, creating significant financial disincentives to accept low paid work. These patterns reveal an important tension in welfare design. More generous benefits tend to create higher participation tax rates unless they are specifically designed to avoid this effect. Less generous benefits create lower participation tax rates but inevitably provide less financial security and higher risks of poverty. This trade-off illustrates a central challenge for basic income implementation, how to balance income security with work incentives. As we examine welfare configurations in the next section, this tension becomes even more apparent when multiple mechanisms interact. The analysis of these configurations advances our broader argument that basic income's effects on job search behaviour cannot be understood by examining isolated principles but rather emerge from complex institutional ecosystems where multiple incentives and disincentives operate simultaneously. Understanding these configurational effects is crucial for predicting how basic income might function across different welfare contexts.

## Welfare Regime Clusters

Clustering of cases or countries is an important element of ideal type research that can help us to identify much about a country's approach to welfare. The basic income ideal type welfare regime has eight distinct ideal types, each representing a unique, but overlapping institutional arrangement of unemployment benefits with differing implications for job search behaviour as well as the potential for basic income implementation.

Different configurations of mechanisms within the unemployment benefits system create distinct incentive structures for job seekers. Based on theoretical and empirical evidence it is possible to estimate their respective incentives. However, certain configurations contain potentially conflicting incentives and disincentives. Take, for example, a welfare regime that combines strict behavioural requirements, high participation tax rates and low accessibility to unemployment benefits. We might hypothesise that this configuration contains two mechanisms which might act as incentives to find work and one which may function as a disincentive. Strict conditionality may increase job search intensity, whilst limited accessibility to unemployment benefits may create financial pressures to accept any available job. However, high participation tax rates might disincentivise job search. This example demonstrates that incentive structures not only overlap but conflict with each other. Such configurations of institutional incentives are central to the interpretation of job search behaviours examined in subsequent chapters.

The following section explores each basic income ideal type, identifying its members and analysing their potential effects on job search behaviour. By examining how different configurations of welfare mechanisms create distinct incentive structures, we can better understand the complex relationship between institutional arrangements and labour market participation. This analysis forms a critical foundation for predicting how a fully implemented basic income might influence job search intensity across varying welfare contexts.

### *Basic Income Ideal Type (Unconditional + Accessible + Low PTR)*

This configuration represents the closest approximation to basic income principles, combining universal, unconditional and non-withdrawable payments. However, no country in the analysis embodies this type, highlighting the departure of existing welfare systems from basic income ideals. The absence of empirical examples highlights the institutional resistance to combining these three principles. This may reflect fundamental tensions in welfare design or political economy constraints that make this combination difficult to sustain within existing institutional frameworks.

The basic income ideal type welfare regime combines an incentive to find work, with two disincentives. In purely theoretical terms it would therefore seem probable that a country with a basic income ideal type welfare regime would demonstrate low job search activity. Unfortunately, the lack of empirical examples limits the ability of this research to conclusively determine whether this is the case. However, the seven other ideal types all contain at least one empirical example, meaning that the research can nevertheless give indications of how a basic income ideal type may impact on job search behaviour.

### *'High PTR' Basic Income Type (Unconditional + Accessible + High PTR)*

Norway is the only example of this configuration, combining unconditionality with accessibility and high participation tax rates. Norway represents a universal, and largely unconditional welfare regime that nonetheless creates significant financial disincentives when transitioning to employment.

In terms of job search behaviour, its high accessibility and low conditionality create an environment with a less prescriptive and pressurised environment for people to undertake job search, potentially enabling better matching between workers and jobs. However, all three conditions represent potentially disincentivising job search mechanisms, with unconditional, easily accessible benefits, combining with high participation tax rates, discouraging unemployed people from accepting lower paid jobs. Overall, we might therefore expect countries in this set to have low levels of job search activity.

### *'Targeted' Basic Income Type (Unconditional + Inaccessible + Low PTR)*

Greece and Spain represent this configuration, combining unconditionality with inaccessibility and low participation tax rates. Whilst Southern European welfare systems have been characterised as underdeveloped (Ferrera, 1996; Leibfried, 2002), their limited conditionality again may provide people with more choice over how to conduct job search activities. Their low participation tax rates, resulting from modest benefit levels, maintain financial incentives to work. However, restricted accessibility means many unemployed individuals receive no institutional support.

This ideal type combines two incentives to find work in being inaccessible and having low participation tax rates, and one disincentive, being unconditional. We may therefore expect cases in this set to have high job search activity.

### *Unconditional Type (Unconditional + Inaccessible + High PTR)*

Belgium is the only member of this ideal type configuration, combining unconditionality with inaccessibility and high participation tax rates. This creates an environment where those who qualify for benefits face minimal behavioural requirements but significant financial disincentives when transitioning into employment. For job seekers who receive benefits, this configuration may enable more selective job search but may also discourage unemployed people from accepting lower paid work.

This ideal type combines two disincentives, low conditionality with high participation tax rates, and one incentive, being low accessibility. Overall, therefore, we might expect countries in this ideal type set to have low job search activity.

### *Participation Income Type (Conditional + Accessible + Low PTR)*

The UK is the only member of this configuration, combining high conditionality with relatively high accessibility and moderate participation tax rates. This creates an environment where benefits are broadly accessible but contingent on continued and demonstrable job search activity.

The UK's approach has a strong 'work first' (Etherington & Daguerre, 2015). It combines strong conditionality to encourage labour market participation, with low participation tax rates, creating both behavioural and financial incentives to find work. Whilst the regime is largely accessible, low flat rate benefit levels, which are paid at the same flat rate for both unemployment insurance and social assistance may contribute to work incentives. This configuration may therefore promote high job search intensity. However, this may come at the cost of pushing people into less suitable work.

This ideal type combines two incentives, being highly conditional with low participation tax rates, with one disincentive, being highly accessible. We would therefore expect cases in this set to have high levels of job search activity.

### *Accessible Type (Conditional + Accessible + High PTR)*

Finland and France are members of this configuration, combining conditionality, accessibility, and high participation tax rates. This balanced approach provides relatively broad access to benefits, maintaining behavioural requirements whilst creating moderate financial disincentives to work. For job seekers, this creates a mixed environment. Whilst benefits are accessible, they are contingent on compliance with job search requirements.

This ideal type represents a combination of one incentive to find work in the form of high conditionality with two disincentives in highly accessible benefits and high participation tax rates. Overall, we might expect cases in this set to have low job search activity.

### *Low PTR Type (Conditional + Inaccessible + Low PTR)*

Italy is the sole representative of this configuration, combining moderate conditionality with limited accessibility and moderate participation tax rates. This creates an environment where benefits are limited in both availability and generosity but maintains financial incentives to work. Italy's welfare approach reflects its familialistic tradition, where limited state support is complemented by family networks (Simonazzi, 2015). For job seekers, this creates pressure to find employment due to limited institutional support, whilst maintaining financial incentives to accept available work.

This ideal type combines three incentives to find work, being highly conditional and inaccessible, with low participation tax rates. Of all the ideal types, we would therefore expect this one to yield cases with high levels of job search activity.

### *Antithesis of Basic Income (Conditional + Inaccessible + High PTR)*

Austria and Germany represent the final configuration, which is the antithesis of basic income, combining moderate conditionality with limited accessibility and high participation tax rates. This creates an ideal type welfare regime that departs from basic income principles in all three dimensions. This approach emphasises insurance based protection with strong conditionality (Esping-Andersen, 1990). For job seekers, this creates a restrictive environment where benefits are contingent on both prior work record and ongoing compliance with job search requirements, whilst creating significant financial disincentives to accept lower paid positions.

This final ideal type is the antithesis of basic income, and combines two incentives, high conditionality and inaccessibility, with one disincentive, high participation tax rates. Overall, the expectation would be that this ideal type produces cases with high levels of job search activity.

## Expectations for Job Search Behaviour

The institutional arrangements identified in the analysis create distinct environments for job seekers, with significant implications for search behaviour and employment outcomes. Norway's 'high PTR basic income' type likely enables selective, autonomous job search but may discourage accepting lower paid positions. This could produce longer but more productive job search periods. The UK's "participation income" type likely produces high job search intensity but limited selectivity. This could lead to shorter unemployment spells but potentially less optimal job matches. Greece and Spain's 'targeted basic income' type creates a dual labour market, those with access to benefits can search more selectively, whilst those without face significant pressure to find any employment.

Table 6.1, summarises the ideal type set memberships and the expectations for job search activity. Subsequent chapters examine whether these expected patterns manifest in actual job search behaviour across these different institutional environments.

The patterns revealed in Table 6.1 represent more than theoretical classifications; they illustrate the complex institutional environments that shape labour market behaviours across Europe. These configurations demonstrate how basic income principles interact with existing welfare structures to create distinct incentive frameworks for job seekers. Rather than assuming uniform impacts across different contexts, the ideal type framework reveals how institutional arrangements mediate basic income principles.

The expectations for job search behaviour outlined in Table 6.1 provide testable hypotheses that will be examined in subsequent chapters using empirical evidence from time use data. By comparing actual job search patterns against these theoretical expectations, we can assess the predictive power of the ideal type framework and better understand how basic income principles influence labour market behaviour in practice. This analysis advances our understanding of basic income beyond abstract theoretical debates by grounding its principles in institutional realities. It suggests that successful basic income implementation would

**Table 6.1** Ideal type set memberships and expectations for job search intensity

| *Narrative description* | *Conditional/ unconditional* | *Accessible/ inaccessible* | *High/low PTR* | *Empirical examples* | *Job search intensity expectation* |
|---|---|---|---|---|---|
| Basic income | Unconditional | Accessible | Low PTR | | Low |
| High PTR basic income | Unconditional | Accessible | High PTR | Norway | Low |
| Targeted Basic income | Unconditional | Inaccessible | Low PTR | Greece Spain | High |
| Unconditional | Unconditional | Inaccessible | High PTR | Belgium | Low |
| Participation income | Conditional | Accessible | Low PTR | UK | High |
| Accessible | Conditional | Accessible | High PTR | Finland France | Low |
| Low PTR | Conditional | Inaccessible | Low PTR | Italy | High |
| Antithesis of basic income | Conditional | Inaccessible | High PTR | Austria Germany | High |

require careful attention to existing welfare configurations and complementary institutional arrangements rather than treating it as a standalone policy solution.

## A Complex Institutional Landscape

The analysis of welfare regimes through the lens of basic income principles reveals the diverse institutional environments that shape job search behaviour across European countries. Whilst no country fully embodies basic income ideals, various welfare configurations approach these principles in different ways, creating distinct incentive structures for unemployed individuals. The patterns identified new configuration of welfare regime typologies whilst providing context for understanding job search behaviour.

The institutional analysis presented in this chapter has identified distinct welfare regime configurations across European countries, each representing different approaches to basic income principles. Having established theoretical expectations about how these configurations might influence job search behaviour, it is instructive to test these predictions against empirical evidence.

This analysis makes several important contributions to both basic income research and welfare regime theory. Firstly, by developing a novel ideal type framework based on basic income principles, it provides a new analytical lens for examining welfare systems that moves beyond traditional welfare regime typologies. Secondly, the identification of eight distinct welfare configurations challenges the notion that welfare systems can be easily classified into just three or four regime types. Instead, the analysis reveals a more complex institutional landscape with multiple hybrid arrangements that combine aspects of different welfare approaches. These findings demonstrate that the path to basic income implementation is not linear but may follow different trajectories depending on existing institutional arrangements. Thirdly, by examining how basic income principles already exist to varying degrees within current welfare regimes, the analysis provides a more realistic foundation for understanding potential transition pathways, highlighting how certain welfare regimes already incorporate aspects of basic income principles, potentially facilitating incremental implementation strategies. Finally, by connecting these institutional configurations to expected job search behaviours, the analysis establishes testable hypotheses about the relationship between welfare design and labour market participation. This moves basic income research beyond abstract theoretical debates towards empirically grounded analysis of how specific institutional arrangements shape behavioural outcomes.

These contributions collectively advance our understanding of how basic income might function across different welfare contexts, providing policymakers with more nuanced frameworks for designing implementation strategies tailored to specific institutional environments.

The next chapter develops a new measure of job search intensity using time use data across the ten European countries analysed here. This approach captures both the frequency and duration of job search activities, revealing how unemployed individuals navigate these different institutional environments. By examining actual job search patterns within each welfare regime type, Chapter 6 provides insights into the relationship between basic income mechanisms and job search behaviours, which are then examined in more depth in part 3 of the book.

## References

Adam, S., Brewer, M., & Shephard, A. (2006). Financial work incentives in Britain: Comparisons over time and between family types. Retrieved April 20, 2024, from https://www.econstor.eu/handle/10419/71567

Anttonen, A. (2012). *Welfare state, universalism and diversity*. Edward Elgar Publishing. Retrieved April 22, 2025, from https://books.google.com/books?hl=en&lr=&id=cgztLxI3onkC&oi=fnd&pg=PP6&dq=Finland+Welfare+regime+universal&ots=tm0r21-65e&sig=JRv5U77vamWe3hC2AdU7ovkyUGM

Esping-Andersen, G. (1990). *The three worlds of welfare capitalism*. Princeton University Press. Retrieved April 22, 2025, from https://books.google.com/books?hl=en&lr=&id=ERCnDwAAQBAJ&oi=fnd&pg=PR8&dq=esping+andersen&ots=0EfqgBd1Qt&sig=1fzL3Snh5oIq8tHHQEAUtM46ZEE

Etherington, D., & Daguerre, A. (2015). *Welfare reform, work first policies and benefit conditionality: Reinforcing poverty and social exclusion*. Centre for Enterprise and Economic Development Research, Middlesex University [Preprint]. Retrieved April 22, 2025, from https://research.thelegaleducationfoundation.org/wp-content/uploads/2017/11/Welfare-and-benefit-conditionality-report-January-2015.pdf

Ferrera, M. (1996). The "Southern Model" of welfare in social Europe. *Journal of European Social Policy, 6*(1), 17–37. https://doi.org/10.1177/095892879600600102

Haagh, L. (2011). Basic income, social democracy and control over time. *Policy & Politics, 39*(1), 43–66.

Kildal, N., & Kuhnle, S. (2007). The Nordic welfare model and the idea of universalism. In *Normative foundations of the welfare state*. Routledge (pp. 25–45). Retrieved April 22, 2025, from https://www.taylorfrancis.com/chapters/edit/10.4324/9780203695241-11/nordic-welfare-model-idea-universalism1-nanna-kildal-stein-kuhnle

Leibfried, S. (2002). Towards a European welfare state? In *New perspectives on the welfare state in Europe* (pp. 128–151). Routledge. Retrieved April 21, 2024, from https://www.taylorfrancis.com/chapters/edit/10.4324/9780203415863-17/towards-european-welfare-state-stephan-leibfried

Martinelli, L. (2017). *'Assessing the case for a Universal Basic Income in the UK', IPR Policy Brief*. University of Bath.

Simonazzi, A. (2015). Italy: Continuity and change in welfare state retrenchment. In *The European social model in crisis* (pp. 339–385). Edward Elgar Publishing. Retrieved April 22, 2025, from https://www.elgaronline.com/edcollchap-oa/book/9781783476565/book-part-9781783476565-13.xml

Torry, M. (2013). *Money for everyone: Why we need a citizen's income*. Policy Press.

CHAPTER 7

# Mapping Job Search Intensity Across European Countries

**Abstract** This chapter develops a measure of job search intensity using time use data across ten European countries, capturing both the frequency and duration of job search activities. The analysis reveals several important patterns that have significant implications for basic income policy and research. Whilst participation in job search activities is generally low across countries there are marked variations in both the frequency and intensity of job searching behaviour across different welfare regimes. The cross-national variations suggest that the relationship between welfare regime types and job search behaviour is complex. The methodology provides a valuable tool which could be used to evaluate future basic income experiments, allowing researchers to observe how basic income shapes job search activity.

**Keywords** Time use data · Job search intensity · Participation rates · Participation time · Cross-national variations · Labour market behaviour · Extensive and intensive margins

This chapter develops a new measure of job search intensity across ten European countries, based on time use data. Unlike traditional employment measures that focus solely on employment outcomes, time use data



S. Watkins, *Basic Income, Work Incentives and Job Search Behaviour*, Exploring the Basic Income Guarantee,
https://doi.org/10.1007/978-3-031-99197-4_7

captures the nuances of how unemployed people spend their time on job search activities, revealing both whether they engage in job search as well as how much time they spend on it. This dual approach enables measures of job search at both the extensive and intensive margins, providing a more detailed picture of job search intensity amongst unemployed people across Europe.

The chapter firstly examines how time use data has been used in previous research, and how time use provides a good measure of job search. It then develops a new measure of job search intensity and applies it to time use data across ten European countries. It finally reports the results of the analysis and summarises the findings and discusses the implications for basic income research.

The findings reveal that whilst participation in job search activities is generally low across countries there are marked variations in both the frequency and intensity of job searching behaviour across different welfare systems. The findings from this chapter form the outcome in the following chapter, which examines the relationship between basic income ideal type welfare regimes and job search intensity.

Job search intensity has proven difficult to measure, with most research either using data from labour force surveys (Green, 2011). Alternative measures have been based on internet search activity (Faberman & Kudlyak, 2019). However, such measures can produce significantly different results, based on how unemployment exit rates or employment entry rates are measured (Baker & Fradkin, 2017). Whilst labour force data captures people's job search activities, detailing the different kinds of activities undertaken to find work, it does not measure the intensity of job search activity. These limitations highlight the need for a direct measure of job search intensity.

## Time Use and Welfare Regimes

Time use surveys represent a unique research method that reveals the intricate patterns of daily life across populations. Surveys provide unparalleled insights into living situations and routines that cannot be captured through other means (Gershuny, 2003). Time use data has become an increasingly important source for economic and social statistics worldwide (Haaramo et al., n.d.), recognised globally as an important measure of living conditions and quality of life (Stiglitz et al., 2009).

Previous research based on time use data reveals significant variations in time use patterns across countries (Charmes, 2015; Fleck, 2009; García Román & Gracia, 2022; Ng & Popkin, 2012; Ortiz-Ospina, Giattino & Roser, 2020) and highlights the importance of recognising the influence of specific institutional and cultural contexts which help perpetuate 'patterns of stratification and differentiation' in society (Gershuny, 2003: 12). Of particular interest to this book is the finding that distinctions between welfare regimes directly impact time allocation. For example, Goodin et al., (2008) observed significant cultural differences between welfare regimes regarding gender roles. In social-democratic societies, such as Finland and Sweden, men share unpaid work because women also occupy highly skilled positions. In contrast, liberal regimes, including Australia and the United States, feature a stark division between high-value jobs and a growing proportion of unskilled positions, leading to specialisation in low-value services and reduced pressure for meaningful changes in gender dynamics.

Gálvez-Muñoz et al. (2011: 141) emphasise that time allocation choices are constrained by social conditions, including institutional environments, noting that 'societal and institutional arrangements encourage different types of family and gender relations'. Additional research has identified varying options for behavioural choices across welfare regimes that affect how time is distributed between paid and unpaid work throughout the life course (Hook & Wolfe, 2012; Neilson & Stanfors, 2014, 2018). Whilst Sullivan et al. (2009) argue that time use data can effectively examine the impact of specific social policies across different national contexts, they also acknowledge the complexity created by multiple policies operating simultaneously within and across nations.

The literature demonstrates that time use data serves as a valuable tool for comparative analysis of macro-level behaviour, capturing time allocations across demographic groups (including unemployed individuals) and examining how these allocations are shaped by institutional, social, and cultural factors.

## Developing a Measure of Job Search Intensity

The research uses microdata from the Harmonised European Time Use Surveys (HETUS) obtained through EUROSTAT. HETUS is a collection of national time use surveys from a range of European countries. There have, so far, been two rounds of HETUS. Round 1 in 2000 collected data between 1998 and 2006. Round 2, in 2010 and upon which this research draws, collected data from 2008 to 2015 (European Union, 2019). The third round is currently under way with around 20 countries completing time use surveys.

Time use surveys record the activities people undertake during a 24 hour period. Data is typically collected during 2 or 3 days over a single week and is collected using time use diaries completed by participants, together with household and individual questionnaires to obtain demographic and additional information on participants and their usual activities. The time use diary consists of 10 or 15 minute time slots into which participants record their activities.

Data can then either be grouped in terms of time of day or types of activity, such as paid work, unpaid household work, or personal care. Harmonisation of HETUS time use surveys is achieved using commonly used variables across countries to maximise comparability (European Union, 2019).

Analysis of the data can be undertaken across two dimensions. Firstly, through identifying daily routines of what activities are undertaken at what points in the day. This gives a rounded picture of how, where, when, and with whom daily activities are undertaken. The second dimension is the aggregating of time spent in different activities, which enables time use data to measure activities at both the intensive and extensive margins. Time use data can also be broken down by geographic and demographic variables, gender, age, and socioeconomic status enabling quantitative analysis of differences in care across these variables.

These aspects of time use data are very important as a measure of job search intensity as they enable measurement of both the extent to which unemployed people participate in job search activities (the participation rate), and how long they spend undertaking them (participation time).

Krueger and Mueller (2010, 2012) identify job search intensity as an important determinant in unemployment status and were the first researchers to use time use data to measure job search intensity, focusing on unemployed people across a range of countries to better understand the relationship between unemployment insurance and unemployment durations, as well as provide a new perspective on the lives of unemployed people. This section builds on their work to develop a new measure of job search intensity.

### *Time Spent in Job Search Activities*

Measuring time spent in job search activities based on time use data provides two dimensions of measurement. The first is the extensive margin, the proportion of people who engage in such activities on given days. This is measured by the *participation rate*, which is the percentage of unemployed people who undertook any job search activities during a diary day, irrespective of how much time they spent doing them. The second measure is the intensive margin, or the amount of time those who undertook job search activities spent on them. This is measured by *participation time*.[1] These two measurements form the core of the job search measure used in this book.

Table 7.1 shows the participation rate and participation time for job search activities amongst unemployed people in each country per day (n is the sample of unemployed people). The sample sizes vary considerably across countries, and it is important to note that small sample sizes, particularly in Norway, may affect the findings from the analysis. As the table shows, both participation rates and time vary significantly, with no correlation between participation rates and participation time.

**Table 7.1** Time use statistics per country

| *Country* | *n* | *Participation rate (%)* | *Participation time (mins)* |
|---|---|---|---|
| Austria | 168 | 18.5 | 128.75 |
| Belgium | 285 | 12.3 | 84.97 |
| Finland | 146 | 8.2 | 50.9 |
| France | 631 | 19 | 90.24 |
| Germany | 349 | 18.6 | 44.91 |
| Greece | 800 | 11.3 | 105.41 |
| Italy | 1214 | 9.1 | 130.3 |
| Norway | 54 | 4.5 | 12.5 |
| Spain | 2053 | 11.1 | 157.24 |
| UK | 245 | 25.2 | 103.33 |
| Average | | 13.78 | 90.86 |

[1] This book focuses on unemployed people between the age of 20–54 when conducting analysis of job search activity to reduce the impact of those heading towards early retirement and of youth unemployment (Krueger and Mueller, 2010, 2012).

**Table 7.2** Summary of time use statistics for 2000 and 2010 HETUS rounds

| *Participation rate (% of unemployed)* | | | |
|---|---|---|---|
| *Case* | *2000 HETUS* | *2010 HETUS* | *Change* |
| Belgium | 4.5 | 10.8 | 6.3 |
| Estonia | 9.8 | 5.5 | − 4.3 |
| Finland | 3.8 | 6.1 | 2.3 |
| France | 16.8 | 15 | − 1.8 |
| Germany | 8.2 | 8.6 | 0.4 |
| Italy | 8.2 | 15.3 | 7.1 |
| Norway | 1.6 | 3.3 | 1.7 |
| Poland | 7.8 | 11.2 | 3.4 |
| Spain | 9.6 | 13.3 | 3.7 |
| UK | 13.4 | 16.4 | 3 |
| Average | 8.37 | 10.55 | |

Source: EUROSTAT

The next step in the analysis is to determine set memberships for each country in either the high or low job search intensity set. The measure is created using the same QCA principles applied in chapter four to establish qualitative cut off points for set membership.

Although Krueger and Mueller (2010, 2012) constructed a similar measure of job search intensity amongst unemployed people, they did not define what constitutes a 'high' or 'low' level of job search intensity. In the absence of prior empirical or theoretical knowledge on which to based calibration of job search intensity, it is necessary instead to examine empirical data and draw conclusions based on this data.

HETUS data is available for the 2000 and 2010 rounds of time use surveys collected across Europe. Table 7.2 shows the participation rate for all countries included in the 2000 and 2010 HETUS rounds. It is useful to examine the overall averages to identify patterns which may provide insight when differentiating high job search intensity from low.

### *Participation Rate*

Daily participation rates are low across all countries included in the analysis. From other studies of job search intensity (Krueger & Mueller, 2010, 2012), we know that this is consistently the case. Krueger and Mueller found that the highest participation rate in their studies was 20.2%, so only 1 in 5 unemployed participate in job search on any given day. In light of these consistent findings, the qualitative cut off point for being in the high job search set should reflect this reality.

The average participation rate increases from 8.37% in the 2000 round to 10.55% in 2010. There is an increase in participation rate in 8 out of the 10 countries for which there is comparable data, suggesting that more people are undertaking job search activities in the 2010 round than in the 2000 round. There may be a variety of reasons for this, from unemployment rates (the 2010 round was largely conducted during the Great Recession, during which unemployment rates were higher than at the turn of the century) to increased behavioural conditionality. However, this question is not within the scope of this book.

Although the definition of unemployed used in this analysis is based solely on self-reported status, it is interesting to consider whether those who did report themselves as searching for a job were actively looking. Using the stricter definition means excluding some countries from the analysis, specifically Germany, Norway, and Spain, where these questions weren't asked, and excluding cases from the other countries where no responses were recorded/there is missing data.

Analysis shows that only including those who reported themselves as unemployed and looking for work yields higher participation rates than including all unemployed. The largest difference is in the UK, where the loose definition of unemployed results in participation rate of 25.2%, whereas the strict definition of unemployed yields a rate of 36.1%, an increase of 10.9 percentage points. A similar increase is evident in Austria, with an increase of 8.8 percentage points from 18.5% to 27.3%. All other countries show far smaller increases. Belgium has an increase of 4.6 percentage points, with the remaining countries showing increases of 2.5 percentage points or lower (See Table 7.3). What we cannot tell from these figures is whether those within the strict definition are in receipt of unemployment benefits. It is not therefore possible to say anything about the impact of benefit receipt, although claimant status has been linked to job search activity, with those in receipt of unemployment benefits having higher job search intensity (Derek, 1990; Faberman & Ismail, 2020).

What we can say is that there appears to be increased participation amongst those who are actively looking for work. However, this is hardly surprising. What it does mean, in terms of calibrating sets, is that to enable inclusion of all 10 countries in the analysis, the calibration of participation

**Table 7.3** Participation rates by unemployment definition

| *Country* | *Self-reported* | | *Self-reported + looking for work* | |
|---|---|---|---|---|
| | *n* | *Participation rate %* | *n* | *Participation rate %* |
| Austria | 130 | 18.5 | 66 | 27.3 |
| Belgium | 203 | 12.3 | 142 | 16.9 |
| Finland | 98 | 8.2 | 59 | 10.2 |
| France | 504 | 19 | 335 | 21.5 |
| Greece | 707 | 11.3 | 556 | 12.8 |
| Italy | 1093 | 9.1 | 1039 | 9.5 |
| UK | 202 | 25.2 | 122 | 36.1 |
| Total/average | 2937 | 14.8 | 2319 | 19.19 |

rate and participation time should be 'loose' enough to allow for differences in unemployment definitions, such that each country would remain in the same set irrespective of the definition used.

Based on this analysis the cut off point for membership in the high job search set for participation rates is set at the average for all cases included in the 2010 HETUS round at 10.5%. This satisfies the condition that the cut off points must be loose enough for participation rates across different definitions of unemployment to be in the same set. The cut off points for being fully out of the high job search set are both set at 0, given there are no particular reasons for setting them at any point higher. The cut off point for being fully in the high job search set for participation rate is set at 50%, being the point at which more unemployed participate in job search than don't.

7 of the 10 cases are in the high job search set for participation rate (Table 7.4). The UK has the highest fuzzy set score, with the continental European countries all in the high job search set, scoring between 0.52 and 0.61. Both Nordic countries are in the low job search set. The southern European countries straddle the cut off point, with both Greece and Spain just in the high job search set (0.51) and Italy in the low job set (0.43).

**Table 7.4** Fuzzy set scores for participation rate

| *Country* | *Participation rate* | *Participation rate fuzzy set score* |
|---|---|---|
| Austria | 18.5 | 0.60 |
| Belgium | 12.3 | 0.52 |
| Finland | 8.2 | 0.38 |
| France | 19 | 0.61 |
| Germany | 18.6 | 0.60 |
| Greece | 11.3 | 0.51 |
| Italy | 9.1 | 0.43 |
| Norway | 4.5 | 0.18 |
| Spain | 11.1 | 0.51 |
| UK | 25.2 | 0.69 |

### *Participation Time*

Although previous measures of job search intensity have focused on participation rates (Krueger & Mueller, 2010, 2012), this research incorporates both participation rates and participation time, measuring job search intensity at the extensive and intensive margins, to gain a more detailed understanding of job search intensity across Europe. Participation time has not previously been included as part of a measure of job search intensity. However, it is an important element of job search intensity, as it is not just the act of undertaking job search, but also how long people engage with it. This is of particular importance when considering the behavioural conditionality requirements in each country. For example, the UK requires that unemployment benefit recipients spend what is equivalent to a full-time job in job search activities. It is therefore interesting to see whether, or to what extent this is reflected in the time use data.

Table 7.5 is a summary of the average participation times for the unemployed across each country in the 2000 and 2010 HETUS rounds.

Although the average time has increased in some countries, particularly the UK, the average increase is 13 minutes amongst countries with data for both rounds, so does represent a large increase.

Figure 7.1 is a histogram of job search participation time[2] and shows that the distribution of participation time is positively skewed to the right.

[2] The histogram includes all data from the 2010 HETUS from all countries included in the analysis.

**Table 7.5** Participation time for 2000 and 2010 HETUS rounds

| *Participation time (minutes per day)* | | | |
|---|---|---|---|
| *Case* | *2000 HETUS round* | *2010 HETUS round* | *Change* |
| Belgium | 81 | 112 | 31 |
| Estonia | 112 | 104 | − 8 |
| France | 105 | 136 | 31 |
| Germany | 89 | 68 | − 21 |
| Italy | 118 | 134 | 16 |
| Poland | 106 | 101 | − 5 |
| Spain | 170 | 158 | − 12 |
| UK | 52 | 123 | 71 |
| Average | 104 | 117 | + 13 |

Source: EUROSTAT

This suggests that using the average (mean) participation time in calibration may place the qualitative cut off point too high in the distribution. In this instance it is better to use the median to guide calibration. The median is 80 minutes per day of job search activity. This represents a more suitable cut off point for membership of the high job search set. Although it is, like the participation rates, quite low. However, as the histogram demonstrates, the proportion of unemployed spending long periods of time in job search activities is very small. Less than 5% of unemployed people across the countries included in the analysis spent 400 minutes (equivalent to 6.67 hours) per day or more in job search activities.

The calibration of participation time also considers the difference between those who self report as 'unemployed' and those who report as 'unemployed' and 'looking for work' in the time use surveys. In contrast to the figures for participation rates, the differences between the unemployed overall, and only those who are reported as actively looking for work are small. The largest difference is around 4 minutes (Table 7.6). What this suggests is that, although the unemployed who report looking for work are more likely to spend time in job search activities, they are not more likely to spend more time in job search activities than the overall unemployed population.

The cut off point for participation time is based on the distribution of job search time, which is very much skewed to the left. 50% of the total sample from all countries included in the analysis spend 80 minute or less per day. The cut off point is set at a more conservative point,

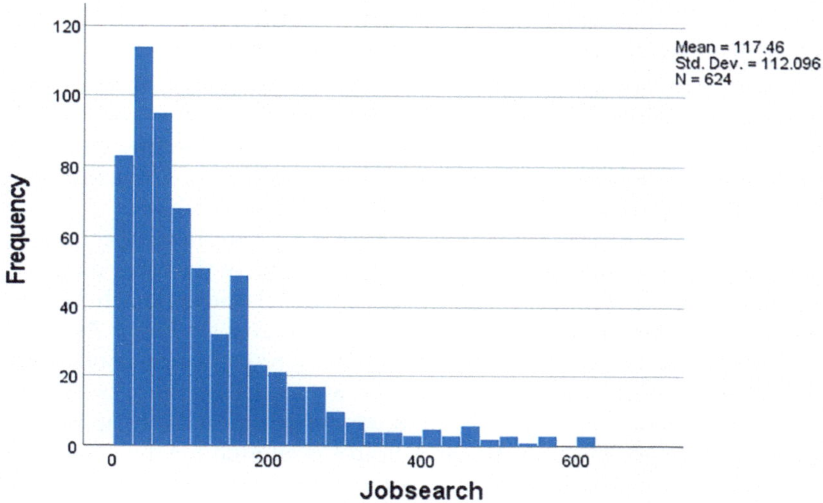


**Fig. 7.1** Histogram of participation time in 10 countries

**Table 7.6** Participation time by unemployment definition

| | *Self-reported* | | *Self-reported + looking for work* | |
|---|---|---|---|---|
| *Country* | *n* | *Participation time* | *n* | *Participation time* |
| Austria | 130 | 128.75 | 66 | 133.33 |
| Belgium | 203 | 84.97 | 142 | 84.94 |
| Finland | 98 | 50.9 | 59 | 47.62 |
| France | 504 | 90.24 | 335 | 86.67 |
| Greece | 707 | 105.41 | 556 | 107.18 |
| Italy | 1093 | 130.3 | 1039 | 130.91 |
| UK | 202 | 103.33 | 122 | 107.44 |
| Total/average | 2937 | 99.13 | 2319 | 99.73 |

being 60 minutes a day. This is also equivalent to spending one 'working' day a week on job search activity (7 hours a day over a 7 day period). Cumulatively, 80% spend less than 3 hours a day in job search activities.

The cut off point for being fully in the high job search set for participation time is therefore set at 3 hours a day (180 minutes).

As with participation rate fuzzy sets, 7 of the 10 cases are in the high job search set (Table 7.7). The Nordic countries are again in the low job search set. The UK is in the high job search set. All continental countries are in the high job search set, with the exception of Germany. The Southern European countries are all in the high job search set.

The final part of the calibration process is to determine the overall; fuzzy set score for job search intensity, based on one of the three methods for combining the secondary level indicators, the classic approach, substitutability, or family resemblance (as discussed in chapter four). As there are only two secondary level indicators, family resemblance is not suitable, so it is either the classic approach, where a case must be in the set for both secondary level indicators, or the substitutability approach, where the presence of only a single indicator is enough for the case to be in the set. The approach taken here is the classic approach, for a case to be in the high job search set, the presence of both high participation rates and participation time are required. This is due to the fact that, although there may be high participation rates, participation time may be very low and vice versa. To be in the set for high job search, high participation rates must be accompanied by high participation time.

**Table 7.7** Participation time fuzzy set scores

| *Country* | *Participation time* | *Participation time fuzzy set score* |
|---|---|---|
| Austria | 128.75 | 0.79 |
| Belgium | 84.97 | 0.60 |
| Finland | 50.9 | 0.42 |
| France | 90.24 | 0.63 |
| Germany | 44.91 | 0.37 |
| Greece | 105.41 | 0.69 |
| Italy | 130.3 | 0.79 |
| Norway | 12.5 | 0.10 |
| Spain | 157.24 | 0.91 |
| UK | 103.33 | 0.68 |

**Table 7.8** Job search intensity fuzzy set scores

| *Country* | *Job search intensity fuzzy set score* |
|---|---|
| Austria | 0.6 |
| Belgium | 0.52 |
| Finland | 0.38 |
| France | 0.61 |
| Germany | 0.37 |
| Greece | 0.51 |
| Italy | 0.43 |
| Norway | 0.1 |
| Spain | 0.51 |
| UK | 0.68 |

### *Fuzzy Set Scores for High Job Search*

Six of the ten cases are in the high job search intensity set. Austria, Belgium, France, Greece, Spain, and the UK are to varying degrees in the high job search intensity set (Table 7.8). The case with the strongest membership is the UK. Belgium, Greece, and Spain are very much borderline cases, with scores very close to the cut off point. The two Nordic countries, together with Germany and Italy, are in the low job search intensity set. Norway, in particular, has very low job search intensity, with a fuzzy set score of 0.10.

## Job Search Intensity Predictions v Expectations

Chapter five concluded with predictions about the expected levels of job search intensity for each basic income ideal type welfare regime, based on theoretical and empirical understanding of the configurations of incentives and disincentives within each configuration. The development of the measure of job search intensity provides an opportunity to revisit the predictions to see whether they match the empirical evidence.

Table 7.9 is an updated version of the table in chapter five, including the empirical findings for each country.

**Table 7.9** Job search intensity predictions v expectations

| *Narrative description* | *Conditional/ unconditional* | *Accessible/ inaccessible* | *High/ low PTR* | *Empirical examples* | *Job search intensity expectation* | *Actual job search intensity* |
|---|---|---|---|---|---|---|
| Basic income | Unconditional | Accessible | Low PTR | | Low | |
| High PTR basic income | Unconditional | Accessible | High PTR | Norway | Low | Low |
| Targeted Basic income | Unconditional | Inaccessible | Low PTR | Greece<br>Spain | High | High<br>High |
| Unconditional | Unconditional | Inaccessible | High PTR | Belgium | Low | High |
| Participation income | Conditional | Accessible | Low PTR | UK | High | High |
| Accessible | Conditional | Accessible | High PTR | Finland<br>France | Low | Low<br>High |
| Low PTR | Conditional | Inaccessible | Low PTR | Italy | High | Low |
| Antithesis of basic income | Conditional | Inaccessible | High PTR | Austria<br>Germany | High | High<br>Low |

## Job Search Intensity and Basic Income Design

The patterns of job search intensity observed across European welfare regimes offer valuable insights for basic income policy design. A key concern in basic income debates is whether unconditional cash transfers might reduce recipients' motivation to seek employment. The data presented in this chapter suggests a nuanced relationship between welfare regime configurations and job search behaviour.

The data reveals important differences between extensive (participation rate) and intensive (participation time) margins of job search. Basic income experiments have typically focused on employment outcomes rather than search processes. However, understanding how basic income might affect both the frequency and intensity of job search activities could help design more effective policies. For instance, future basic income experiments might wish to consider whether basic income enables more strategic job searching rather than measuring only aggregate search time.

Significant cross-national variations suggest that basic income's effects on job search behaviour may depend heavily on existing labour market institutions and cultural contexts. The relatively low job search intensity in Nordic countries, despite their strong employment outcomes, strongly suggests that other factors such as active labour market policies, job quality, and social norms around work may be important determinants of employment outcomes.

## Implications for Basic Income Research

The methodology and findings presented in this chapter have significant implications for basic income research design and evaluation. Time use data offers unique advantages for understanding how basic income might affect job seeking behaviour—an aspect often oversimplified in basic income debates.

First, this methodology could enhance evaluation of existing basic income experiments. Most experiments currently focus on binary employment outcomes. By incorporating time use measurements, researchers could capture more nuanced behavioural changes. For example, time use data could reveal whether basic income recipients engage in more targeted job searching, spend more time researching potential employers, or allocate more time to skill development alongside job seeking. This granular data would help address concerns about whether basic income affects not just employment outcomes, but the quality of job matches.

The cross-national variations in job search patterns identified here also suggest important considerations for future basic income experiment design. The substantial differences between Nordic and other European countries indicate that experimental studies need to carefully account for existing labour market institutions and cultural contexts. Future experiments might benefit from:

Parallel measurement approaches that combine traditional employment metrics with time use data to capture both outcomes and behavioural changes

Longer observation periods to understand how job search patterns evolve as participants adjust to unconditional income support

Comparative experiments across different welfare regime contexts to understand how existing institutional arrangements influence basic income's effects

The fuzzy set methodology developed here could be particularly valuable for monitoring long-term basic income implementation. By establishing baseline measures of job search intensity across different welfare systems, researchers could track how these patterns shift during transition to basic income. This would help identify whether initial changes in job search behaviour persist or evolve over time.

However, the findings also highlight important methodological challenges for basic income research. The low overall rates of job search activity suggest that large sample sizes may be needed to detect significant changes in behaviour. Additionally, the distinction between participation rates and participation time indicates that basic income evaluations need to measure both the extensive and intensive margins of job search activity.

These insights point to several priorities for future research:

- Development of standardised time use measurements for basic income pilots to enable cross-study comparison
- Investigation of how online job searching and remote work opportunities might affect the relationship between income security and job search behaviour
- Analysis of how different basic income levels might affect job search intensity, particularly given the varying patterns observed across welfare regimes with different benefit levels
- Examination of potential interaction effects between basic income and other labour market policies, such as job search assistance or training programmes

This methodological framework provides a foundation for more sophisticated analysis of how basic income might influence labour market behaviour, moving beyond simple assumptions about work incentives to understand the complex ways in which income security shapes job search strategies.

## A New Measure of Job Search Intensity Across Welfare Regimes

This chapter has developed and applied a new measure of job search intensity across European welfare regimes using time use data. Whilst participation in job search activities is generally low across countries, there are marked variations in both the frequency and intensity of job searching behaviour across different welfare systems.

The methodology developed here, combining both extensive (participation rate) and intensive (participation time) measures of job search, provides valuable tools for future basic income research. Time use data offers unique insights into how people conduct their job search, potentially revealing qualitative changes in job seeking strategies that might result from enhanced income security. This could be particularly valuable for evaluating basic income experiments, enabling researchers to capture subtle behavioural changes overlooked by traditional employment metrics.

However, the findings also highlight important complexities in measuring and interpreting job search behaviour. The generally low levels of recorded job search activity suggest that large sample sizes may be needed to detect significant effects in basic income experiments. Additionally, the variation across welfare regimes indicates that basic income's effects on job search behaviour may depend heavily on existing labour market institutions and cultural contexts.

These insights suggest that future basic income research and policy design should consider not just whether people search for jobs, but how they conduct their search when provided with income security. Understanding these behavioural patterns could help design basic income policies that support both individual welfare and labour market functioning.

Part Three of this book moves from theoretical concepts to empirical analysis and practical policy implications of basic income. It applies our analytical frameworks to examine actual behavioural patterns across European welfare systems and extrapolates findings for basic income implementation.

Chapter Eight presents empirical analysis using fuzzy set qualitative comparative analysis (QCA) to identify relationships between welfare mechanisms and job search intensity across ten European countries. The findings challenge conventional assumptions about work incentives, revealing that supposedly incentivising welfare mechanisms have limited impact on job search behaviour. Chapter Nine examines these empirical findings' implications for basic income policy through counterfactual analysis, exploring how identical basic income schemes might function differently within contrasting welfare contexts, specifically Finland and the UK. Rather than viewing basic income as inherently incentivising work, this analysis reconceptualizes it as enhancing income security within specific institutional frameworks. Chapter Ten synthesises the book's insights, highlighting key lessons for research and policy development. It emphasises how institutional contexts mediate welfare effects, challenges assumptions about work incentives, and outlines promising directions for future inquiry and policy implementation.

Together, these chapters demonstrate that basic income's effects are neither linear nor deterministic but emerge from complex interactions between policy mechanisms, institutional contexts, and individual responses. By grounding predictions in evidence rather than assumptions, Part Three provides a foundation for more realistic expectations and more effective implementation strategies.

## References


Baker, S. R., & Fradkin, A. (2017). The impact of unemployment insurance on job search: Evidence from Google search data. *Review of Economics and Statistics, 99*(5), 756–768.

Charmes, J. (2015). Time use across the world: Findings of a world compilation of time use surveys. *Background paper for human development report* [Preprint]. Retrieved April 22, 2025, from https://www.researchgate.net/profile/Jacques-Charmes/publication/307199664_Time_Use_Across_the_World_Findings_of_a_World_Compilation_of_Time_Use_Surveys/links/57c4369f08aee50192e88891/Time-Use-Across-the-World-Findings-of-a-World-Compilation-of-Time-Use-Surveys.pdf

Derek, L. B. (1990). Unemployment and the intensity and method of job search. *International Journal of Manpower, 11*(1). Retrieved January 25, 2024, from https://elibrary.ru/item.asp?id=6482622

European Union. (2019). *Harmonised European Time Use Surveys (HETUS) 2018 guidelines*. Publications Office of the European Union Luxembourg.

Faberman, R. J., & Ismail, A. H. (2020). How do unemployment benefits relate to job search behavior. *Chicago Fed Letter, 441*, 1–6.

Faberman, R. J., & Kudlyak, M. (2019). The intensity of job search and search duration. *American Economic Journal: Macroeconomics, 11*(3), 327–357.

Fleck, S. E. (2009). International comparisons of hours worked: An assessment of the statistics. *Monthly Labor Review, 132*, 3.

Gálvez-Muñoz, L., Rodríguez-Modroño, P., & Domínguez-Serrano, M. (2011). Work and time use by gender: A new clustering of European welfare systems. *Feminist Economics, 17*(4), 125–157. https://doi.org/10.1080/13545701.2011.620975

García Román, J., & Gracia, P. (2022). Gender differences in time use across age groups: A study of ten industrialized countries, 2005–2015. *PLoS ONE, 17*(3), e0264411.

Gershuny, J. (2003). *Changing times: Work and leisure in postindustrial society*. Oxford University Press.

Goodin, R. E., et al. (2008). Discretionary time: A new measure of freedom. Retrieved April 8, 2025, from https://philpapers.org/rec/GOODTA

Green, A. E. (2011). *Job search study: Literature review and analysis of the labour force survey*. Corporate Document Services.

Haaramo, J., Pääkkönen, H., & Niemi, I. (n.d.). (2024, January 22). A road full of challenges: How time use surveys became an essential part of statistical production. *Time Reveals Everything van Tienoven, Theun Pieter; Minnen, Joeri; Spruyt, Bram*. Retrieved 22 January 2024. https://aspeditions.be/asp_mailing/Time_reveals_everything/10.46944978946l175229.5.pdf

Hook, J. L., & Wolfe, C. M. (2012). New fathers? Residential fathers' time with children in four countries. *Journal of Family Issues, 33*(4), 415–450. https://doi.org/10.1177/0192513X11425779

Krueger, A. B., & Mueller, A. (2010). Job search and unemployment insurance: New evidence from time use data. *Journal of Public Economics, 94*(3–4), 298–307.

Krueger, A. B., & Mueller, A. I. (2012). The lot of the unemployed: A time use perspective. *Journal of the European Economic Association, 10*(4), 765–794.

Neilson, J., & Stanfors, M. (2014). It's about time! gender, parenthood, and household divisions of labor under different welfare regimes. *Journal of Family Issues, 35*(8), 1066–1088.

Neilson, J., & Stanfors, M. (2018). Time alone or together? Trends and trade-offs among dual–earner couples, Sweden 1990–2010. *Journal of Marriage and Family, 80*(1), 80–98. https://doi.org/10.1111/jomf.12414

Ng, S. W., & Popkin, B. M. (2012). Time use and physical activity: A shift away from movement across the globe. *Obesity Reviews, 13*(8), 659–680. https://doi.org/10.1111/j.1467-789X.2011.00982.x

Ortiz-Ospina, E., Giattino, C., & Roser, M. (2020). Time use. *Our World in Data* [Preprint]. Retrieved April 22, 2025, from https://ourworldindata.org/time-use

Stiglitz, J. E., Sen, A., & Fitoussi, J. P. (2009). *Report by the commission on the measurement of economic performance and social progress*. The Commission Paris. https://www.cbs.nl/-/media/imported/documents/2011/36/stiglitzsenfitoussireport_2009.pdf

Sullivan, O., Coltrane, S., Mcannally, L., & Altintas, E. (2009). Father-friendly policies and time-use data in a cross-national context: Potential and prospects for future research. *The ANNALS of the American Academy of Political and Social Science, 624*(1), 234–254. https://doi.org/10.1177/0002716209335138

# Part III

CHAPTER 8

# Incentives and Disincentives: Analysing Welfare Mechanisms' Effects on Job Search Behaviour

**Abstract** This chapter bridges theory and empirical evidence by analysing the relationship between basic income welfare mechanisms and job search activities amongst unemployed people across ten European countries. Using fuzzy set qualitative comparative analysis (QCA), the analysis examines behaviours under a variety of welfare conditions. The analysis focuses on three key conditions: conditionality, accessibility, and participation tax rates. The findings reveal that work incentives have limited impact on job search intensity, whilst a specific combination of welfare conditions prove sufficient for low job search activity. The results highlight the importance of institutional context, administrative approaches, and complex causality in understanding how welfare systems influence labour market behaviours. The chapter offers important insights for basic income policy design by demonstrating that the behavioural effects of welfare mechanisms are neither linear nor deterministic but emerge from complex interactions within specific welfare ecosystems.

**Keywords** Necessary and sufficient conditions · Work first approach · Human capital approach · Administration of conditionality · Benefit duration and generosity · Causal asymmetry · Conjunctural causation



S. Watkins, *Basic Income, Work Incentives and Job Search Behaviour*, Exploring the Basic Income Guarantee,
https://doi.org/10.1007/978-3-031-99197-4_8

This chapter combines the measures of job search intensity and the basic income ideal type welfare regimes to analyse how different welfare configurations impact on job search behaviour across European countries. It focuses on the incentives and disincentives to find work that are, theoretically at least, inherent within the principles that define basic income. The concept of basic income has generated significant debate centring on its potential effects on work motivation and labour market participation. These debates are based on perceptions of the effects of the principles that underpin basic income. Critics argue that removing conditionality from welfare benefits would inevitably reduce work effort (Minogue, 2018, White, 2023), whilst proponents suggest that reducing marginal tax rates on employment transitions would enhance work incentives (Torry, 2018). Both perspectives typically rely on relatively straightforward assumptions about how specific welfare mechanisms influence behaviour. This chapter tests these assumptions empirically, examining how different welfare configurations actually relate to observed job search behaviours.

The analysis uses fuzzy set qualitative comparative analysis (QCA) to identify necessary and sufficient conditions for high and low job search intensity across ten European countries. This methodology is well suited to investigating complex causal relationships where outcomes may result from different combinations of conditions rather than isolated factors. By examining welfare systems as configurations of interdependent conditions the analysis helps to capture the complex institutional realities into which basic income would be introduced.

The analysis includes three basic income principles, configured and measured as welfare mechanisms: conditionality, accessibility, and participation tax rates. By identifying which welfare configurations are associated with higher or lower job search intensity, this chapter provides empirical grounding for debates that have often relied more on theoretical assumptions than empirical evidence. The findings challenge conventional wisdom about welfare incentives and highlight the complex, configurational nature of how welfare regimes influence job search behaviour.

The chapter firstly outlines the QCA methodology and defines the key conditions examined. It then presents the empirical results, identifying necessary and sufficient conditions for both high and low job search intensity. The next section explores case studies to identify potential causal mechanisms underlying these findings, examining welfare administration approaches, and benefit duration and generosity. Finally, the chapter discusses implications for basic income design, highlighting how institutional context and implementation may prove more influential than specific policy mechanisms in determining behavioural outcomes.

## Identifying Necessary and Sufficient Conditions for High and Low Job Search Intensity

This section is a fuzzy set qualitative comparative analysis of job search intensity across 10 European countries.

### *The QCA Model*

The three conditions included in the model are:

- Conditional (C)
- Accessible (A)
- High participation tax rates (T)

The outcome is a measure of job search intensity levels by unemployed people across each country. The measure is based on time use data from each country, pooled to represent the average unemployed person's time spent in job search activities.

Table 8.1 shows the QCA model, including the 10 European cases, their set scores for Conditional (C), Accessible (A), and High Participation Tax Rate (T), together with the outcome scores for the High Job Search outcome ("HJS"). A fuzzy set QCA is then used to establish whether certain configurations of welfare regimes are necessary or sufficient for the presence of high job search intensity.

The main purpose of QCA is to determine whether specific conditions are necessary or sufficient for the outcome. The next section contains the results of the fuzzy set QCA, which tests the necessity and sufficiency of the conditions, behavioural conditionality, participation tax rates, and accessibility for the outcomes of high job search and low job search.

### *Results of the Fuzzy Set QCA*

The QCA model tested two separate outcomes, high and low job search intensity to determine whether the conditions included in the model were either necessary or sufficient for the presence of either of these outcomes.

**Table 8.1** The QCA model

| *Case no* | *Country* | *C* | *A* | *T* | *HJS* |
|---|---|---|---|---|---|
| 1 | Austria | 0.54 | 0.45 | 0.66 | 0.60 |
| 2 | Belgium | 0.45 | 0.32 | 0.66 | 0.52 |
| 3 | Finland | 0.61 | 0.66 | 0.59 | 0.38 |
| 4 | France | 0.51 | 0.57 | 0.59 | 0.61 |
| 5 | Germany | 0.60 | 0.45 | 0.60 | 0.37 |
| 6 | Greece | 0.28 | 0.00 | 0.20 | 0.51 |
| 7 | Italy | 0.52 | 0.49 | 0.47 | 0.43 |
| 8 | Norway | 0.44 | 0.96 | 0.60 | 0.10 |
| 9 | Spain | 0.47 | 0.45 | 0.41 | 0.51 |
| 10 | UK | 0.98 | 0.69 | 0.47 | 0.68 |

*High Job Search Intensity*

None of the conditions, either individually or in combination were either necessary or sufficient for the presence of high job search. This confounds expectations about conditions thought to be incentivising, namely high conditionality, low participation tax rates, and low accessibility. The one empirical example that combined these three conditions is Italy, which itself is in the low job search intensity set. The QCA provides no evidence that the supposed work incentives have any impact on job search intensity at the aggregate level.

The analysis reveals a contradiction between theoretical expectations and empirical findings regarding job search intensity across different welfare regimes. Theoretically, there should be clear relationships between policy mechanisms and behavioural outcomes: high conditionality should compel greater job search effort (McVicar, 2008; Johnson & Klepinger, 1994; Dolton & O'Neill, 2002; Gorter & Kalb, 1996; Setty, 2019); low participation tax rates should encourage job seeking; as should limiting access to generous benefits (Corsini, 2013; Filiz, 2017; Le Barbanchon, 2013; Vodopivec et al., 2015). Yet the QCA analysis found that none of these conditions, either individually or in combination, proved necessary or sufficient for high job search intensity. These findings are significant for basic income debates. Critics of basic income frequently argue that removing conditionality would inevitably reduce work motivation, whilst proponents suggest that reducing marginal rates of tax on moving into work would enhance work incentives. The findings challenge both positions, suggesting that the relationship between welfare design and job search behaviour is far more complex than either side typically acknowledges.

*Low Job Search Intensity*
No conditions were found to be necessary for the presence of low job search intensity. However, the analysis identified a combination of two conditions as sufficient for the presence of low job search intensity, high participation tax rate, and high accessibility.

The two Nordic countries, Finland and Norway, were 'typical' of this configuration and were also members of the low job search set. The presence of typical countries helps to bolster the robustness of the findings. However, there are also countries which contradict this finding in France, Germany, and Italy. France is a member of both the high participation tax rate set and the accessible set and therefore should also be a member of the low job search set. However, it is not. In contrast, Germany and Italy are both members of the low job search intensity set, but not the condition sets.

Just as typical cases increase the robustness of the findings, deviant cases reduce it. There are several tests of robustness available to researchers using QCA, and these were applied to the QCA model. The model scored well in the robustness tests (which are available on request to the author), so there is good reason to conclude that the combination of high participation tax rates and accessibility are sufficient for the presence of low job search intensity.

An integral part of QCA is understanding the mechanisms which underpin the conditions, leading to the specified outcomes. For a QCA analysis to make sense, there should be an underlying theoretical reasoning which links the conditions to the outcome (Schneider & Wagemann, 2012). In this instance, both causal conditions identified as sufficient for the presence of low job search are theoretically disincentives to undertake job search activities. High participation tax rates provide a financial disincentive to job search, as the unemployed benefit recipient is little or no better off when moving from unemployment into employment. High accessibility, particularly to generous unemployment insurance schemes, provides a guaranteed income for a defined period, and may therefore reduce the need to find work in the short term. However, it is important to note that neither condition was sufficient in isolation, and only the two conditions combined were found to be sufficient for the presence of low job search, demonstrating the complex causal pathways between basic income principles and job search behaviour.

### *Basic Income and Causal Complexity*

These findings demonstrate two important elements that are key to the methodological approach adopted in this book that relate to causal complexity.

The first is conjunctural causation where the effects of a single condition can only be seen when combined with other conditions (Ragin, 2014). The QCA analysis found that high participation tax rates and highly accessible benefits were sufficient for the presence of low job search intensity only when both were present, demonstrating that causal pathways to outcomes are complex and depend on the interdependence of conditions.

The second is causal asymmetry, which describes the way in which insights on the causal role of a condition help to explain the presence of an outcome but are of little use in explaining its absence (Mahoney, 2008). The QCA did not identify any causal conditions necessary or sufficient for the presence of high job search intensity, but the combined presence of high participation tax rates and highly accessible benefits was found to be sufficient for the presence of low job search intensity. This suggests that whilst low participation tax rates and inaccessible benefits do not act as an incentive to find work, high participation tax rates and highly accessible benefits may act as a disincentive to find work. This highlights the causal asymmetry where the role and significance of conditions differ in relation to the outcome and its absence. The conclusion that could be drawn here is that whilst some factors may act as a disincentive to find work, their removal or antithesis does not necessarily create an incentive to find work.

When undertaking a QCA with a small number of cases, post-QCA case studies are commonly used to examine potential underlying causal mechanisms that may help to explain the findings from the QCA analysis (Schneider & Rohlfing, 2013). The following section undertakes a series of case studies to identify potential underlying causal mechanisms.

The first case study examines the conditional condition to identify why it was not found to be necessary or sufficient for the presence of high job search as hypothesised and whether additional administrative factors may help to explain variations in job search intensity. The second case study addresses the sufficiency term High participation tax rate and Accessible, focusing on the duration and generosity of unemployment benefits, which may be underlying causal factors in job search intensity.

## Case Study 1: The Administration of Conditionality

This case study examines the policies and administrative tools that combine to produce conditionality at 'street level'. It investigates how welfare regimes prioritise the requirement for unemployed people to find employment in the short term or focus more on long term employment through skills development.

Two main strategies for approaching conditionality have been identified in the literature. The first is an institutional 'work first' emphasis (Levy, 2004; Minas, 2014; Peck & Theodore, 2000), which stresses the importance of paid work over and above any other considerations such as long term training, health, or educational needs. The main focus of these institutions is to move people from unemployment into employment, irrespective of long term suitability of the employment (Clasen and Clegg, 2011). Both Germany and the UK exemplify this approach, although with significant differences in implementation. The second approach is the 'human capital' approach, characterised by an emphasis on enhancing skills, training, and work placements. It has a more holistic approach to unemployment and considers other aspects of the individual circumstances of the unemployed, such as skill development, health, education, and familial needs. Finland and Norway both fall into the 'human capital' category (Levy, 2004; Minas, 2014).

Job centres play a central role in both approaches, albeit in very different ways. In work first environments job centres are characterised by the narrowness of the provisions offered, focusing specifically on employment outcomes. Other services are largely separate or periphery (Wiggan, 2007). In contrast, the 'human capital' job centre has more to offer in terms of training and additional health or other services (Minas, 2014).

### *Work First Policy and Administration*

UK Jobcentres have a narrow, 'work first' organisational remit, to get people into work as quickly as possible (Boland, 2016). They are responsible for processing newly unemployed applications, as well as determining benefits and imposing sanctions.

The emphasis on getting the unemployed back into work is supported by the strict behavioural requirements in place designed to regulate the behaviour of the unemployed as they seek to find work, in particular job search activity requirements. Recipients of unemployment benefits are allocated a 'Work Services Coach' who sets work search activities for claimants to undertake, based on an expectation of spending 35 hours per week in work search activities.[1] The unemployed are therefore expected to treat job search activities as a full-time commitment. This requirement is far more onerous than in any of the other countries in the study. UK jobcentres are also provided with financial incentives for placing unemployed people into work (Wiggan, 2007), further increasing their 'work first' approach.

Monitoring the behaviour of the unemployed is also strict, with fortnightly 'Job Search Reviews'. These provide case workers with regular opportunities to ensure people are actively seeking work and remain entitled to benefits. During Job search reviews case workers discuss the unemployed person's job search activity, using the 'Job Search Agreement', an integration contract used to establish their job goals, review the steps they agreed to take including asking what steps they have taken to look for work. Evidence collected is then logged on to the system to show that eligibility has been met.

The UK is a good example of the integration of strict behavioural conditions, combined with strong 'work first' orientation, where the emphasis is on intensive job search and participation in short term training or work-experience (Clasen and Clegg, 2011), placing the UK at the top of the league of countries that place increasing the pressure on benefit claimants to find paid work (Daguerre & Etherington, 2009).

Perhaps the single greatest difference between the UK and the rest of the cases in terms of conditionality, is the requirement to treat job search as equivalent to a full-time job (CPAG, 2015). In comparison there is

[1] Less any time spent undertaking agreed work preparation activities, voluntary work and paid work (CPAG, 2015).

no other country that makes such demands. Although job search activity rates are higher in the UK than any other case, the actual time recorded in time use surveys by the unemployed is nowhere near what is required, bringing into question the need or effectiveness of such a policy. From the sample of 245 unemployed people in the UK time use data, only three recorded job search activity of more than 4 hours per day. Of those people who undertook job search almost 70% spent less than an hour on it, another 25% less than 2 hours and another 20% under 3 hours in job search activities. This is significant when considering how much is expected of unemployed people in the UK who wish to retain access to unemployment benefits, for fear of being sanctioned and benefits withdrawn. The presence of such demanding job search criteria, combined with a strong 'work first' administration is suggestive of the presence of a causal mechanism linking high conditional scores to high job search scores. To examine this further it is important to see whether another example of a work first administration also results in high job search intensity.

Germany also combines a 'work first' orientation with strong behavioural conditionality. In contrast to the UK, the administration of benefits is split between two tiers, the main unemployment insurance scheme, 'UBI' (not to be confused with universal basic income), is administered by the national PES (job centres), whereas the second tier of benefits 'UBII', is administered by municipalities. Despite the differences in administration, there is a large degree of similarity in terms of the conditionality imposed on recipients of each (Dingeldey, 2011).

Integration contracts are, as in the UK, compulsory for unemployed benefit recipients, setting out each individual's job search strategy which must be updated regularly or adapted to changes that occur. The strategy requires the unemployed person to intensively look for a new job. However, unlike the UK, in Germany there is no binding requirement to furnish evidence of the person's own efforts, nor is there a minimum time requirement that the unemployed person is required to spend in looking for work. This is an important distinction between the two countries. Although the focus of German job centres is work first, there is far less compulsion in the German system.

The lack of compulsion in terms of time spent may help to explain low job search activities in Germany when compared to the high levels in the UK. However, it is important to note that none of the other countries in the study have such onerous job search activity requirements as the UK, yet many still have high levels of job search intensity. Whilst these rules may have an impact on job search activity in the UK, their absence from other cases with high job search does not suggest that their presence is necessary for high job search activities. They may be sufficient, although the QCA did not observe this. Further analysis, with more examples of cases with such high levels of required job search activity, is required to test this hypothesis.

### *Human Capital Policy and Administration*

By comparison with jobcentres in 'work first' welfare regimes, Nordic jobcentres are more multipurpose, with a more human capital approach that relies on training and other competence-building activities, in addition to requirements to actively seek employment. These multipurpose one-stop shops reflect the ambition to invest in prevention and in human and social capital. Traditionally, this has been seen as a Nordic approach to activation exemplified by Finland and Norway (Minas, 2014).

Although the activation trend seen across Europe in the last two decades has permeated the Nordic countries too, reforms to (un)employment policies have deviated from the 'work first' emphasis of other countries. Instead, Nordic countries have developed a more comprehensive form of support for the unemployed, with an emphasis on training to get people back into work, rather than getting people into the first job that becomes available. In Finland, clients of the employment service are offered a range of personalised services, such as health services, and activities for developing everyday life skills, education and practical training (Karjalainen & Saikku, 2011).

Finland is in the high conditionality set but low job search set. In contrast to the UK, Finland's administration is much more varied, encompassing multiple professional services, including social services, voluntary organisations and private companies, in addition to employment services provided by the municipality itself. These cover several policy sectors, assessing a broad variety of needs. Finnish employment services, like the German versions, have more leeway for organising operations at a local level (Karjalainen & Saikku, 2011). There is much more local autonomy, with a network design at the local level based on contracts between the local authorities and employment offices, in contrast to the centrally managed, top-down approach in the UK.

Much like Germany and the UK, integration plans are used, which agree on the job seeking activities required. However, there is no compulsion for it to be agreed immediately, only after 5 months of unemployment does it become compulsory. Monitoring of job search activity is much lighter than in the UK. It is usually sufficient for the jobseeker to inform the job centre that agreed actions have been accomplished. However, the integration plan may include an agreement that other evidence is required, such as copies of job applications, suggesting a higher level of discretion than in the UK.

Norway is in both the low conditionality and low job search sets. It is also the best example of a human capital strategy to unemployment integration. Over the past twenty years, the activation paradigm has been prevalent in Norway. Reforms have nevertheless strayed from other countries' work first priorities. A major concern for the Norwegian job centres is the need for more comprehensive help for the unemployed, in addition to raising activation rates. Job seekers in Norway can choose between individualised health treatments, combinations of services for specific needs, group activities for developing social and living skills, education, and hands-on training (Minas, 2014). In addition to increasing activation rates, the Norwegian system seeks to offer more comprehensive support to the unemployed. Although sanctions are imposed for failures to comply with behavioural requirements, meaning that Norway is not entirely unconditional, it is, overall, less conditional, in terms of behavioural requirements for the unemployed, and monitoring, than other countries included in the analysis.

Although the unemployed in Norway are required to evidence job search activity, there is no set period during which this must be done, unlike other countries such as the UK which stipulates that this must be done every two weeks. There are also no minimum job search activity requirements specified. Norway is an example of low conditionality, combined with a human capital approach and is in the low job search activity set. The lack of strong conditionality, combined with strong human capital approach may be sufficient for the presence of low job search activity.

The findings of the case study suggest a nuanced relationship between welfare conditionality policy, administration, and job search activity in the countries studied. It was hypothesised that more intrusive and demanding forms of administrations should result in higher levels of job search, by extension it stands to reason that less demanding and intrusive forms of conditionality would result in lower levels of conditionality. The UK supports this hypothesis, and the case study suggests that the combination of a 'work first' approach and demanding job search criteria may combine to produce high job search intensity. However, despite being in the high conditionality set and adopting a 'work first' approach, Germany exhibits low job search intensity. This suggests that high levels of conditionality and a 'work first' administration are not sufficient for high job search.

The Norwegian model suggests that low conditionality and a human capital approach might lead to low job search. The absence of strong conditionality combined with a focus on human capital may be sufficient for low job search intensity. However, Finland, which also has low job search and a human capital approach to the administration of conditionality is in the highly conditional set. This suggests that a human capital approach may mediate job search behaviour. Whilst the hypothesis provides a general framework, specific policy details, the interplay of conditionality and administration, and the unique mechanisms in each country contribute to varied outcomes in job search intensity. The cases emphasise the importance of specific institutional and social contexts in understanding the specific elements influencing the relationship between conditionality, administration, and job search.

## Case Study 2: Accessibility to First Tier Unemployment Benefits and Measures of Duration and Generosity

The measure of accessibility is based on two forms of unemployment benefits. Unemployment insurance pays benefits for a specified duration (except in Belgium) and, with the exception of the UK, is based on levels of previous earnings. The second type is unemployment/social assistance benefits, which are means-tested, flat rate benefits, paid without a limited duration. This section examines the varying degrees of generosity and duration of unemployment insurance payments, which may be a mediating factor in determining job search intensity in cases with high or low accessibility.

Standard job theory links longer periods of unemployment with extended periods of benefit duration, which have the effect of reducing the level of effort spent on job search and/or increases people's reservation wage, which is the lowest wage at which an individual will accept paid work (Lichter, 2016). There is evidence that unemployment insurance has a disincentivising effect on labour market participation, which may be mediated by both the generosity of benefits and the potential benefit duration. Studies have shown that extending the duration of unemployment insurance payments increases periods of unemployment, regardless of their personal characteristics or the job market (see Card & Levine, 2000; Chetty, 2008; Katz & Meyer, 1990; Lalive et al., 2006; Schmieder et al., 2012; Van Ours & Vodopivec, 2006) and that increased benefit generosity increases the period of unemployment (Marie & Castello, 2012; Vodopivec et al., 2015). Although none of the evidence cited above directly examines job search activity, extended periods of unemployment may be suggestive of lower levels of job search activity, suggesting a link between benefit generosity and duration and job search intensity.

Except for Belgium, unemployment insurance benefits amongst countries in the study are paid for a set period, ranging from 17 to 104 weeks. Except for the UK, unemployment insurance benefits are also based on a percentage of previous earnings. It is therefore possible to scope out the overall duration and generosity for each household type across the countries included in the study.

The measure of generosity used here is based on average 'net replacement rate'.[2] Net replacement rate ('NRR') is defined as the ratio of net income whilst unemployed, divided by net income whilst in work. Replacement rates provide an indication of the level of lost income from work that is compensated by benefits. Lower net replacement rates are associated with a greater incentive to search for and take up a job when unemployed. (Allan & Scruggs, 2004; Esping-Andersen, 1990; Korpi & Palme, 2003). In this sense they are similar to the measure of participation tax rates used in the QCA. The main difference is that NRR measures what percentage of working income is maintained when unemployed, whilst PTR measures what percentage of additional earnings is effectively lost through taxes and benefit reductions when moving from unemployment to employment.

[2] Published by the OECD (OECD.org,c) and EUROSTAT (EUROSTAT,b).

It should be noted that there is no universal replacement rate in any country. Instead, there exist numerous replacement rates that are determined by the individual and family characteristics of the unemployed, their employment and unemployment history, and the various structures and benefits provided by unemployment insurance and social assistance systems. These systems also interact with tax systems, further influencing the replacement rates. Attempting to comprehend these intricacies to calculate replacement rates for the sake of worldwide comparisons is a formidable undertaking. Instead, what is presented here is a 'country profile' with averages used to denote high or low levels of replacement rates (Van Vliet & Caminada, 2012). In Table 8.2, generosity is measured by NNR and duration by number of weeks.

In the absence of theoretical or other empirical measures which may help to identify natural cut off points for identifying in the absence of theoretical or other empirical measures which may help to identify natural cut off points for identifying high or low generosity and short or long duration and high or low generosity, the median of each is used as a cut off point for determining high and low levels of duration (60.5) and generosity (65.05). Of the countries included in the case studies, France, Finland, and Norway have both high generosity and long duration. Of the other two cases, Germany has high duration but low generosity, and the UK has both low generosity and short duration.

Finland and Norway are in the high accessibility and low job search set. The presence of long duration and high generosity in these two cases supports the hypothesis that a combination of the two may produce low job search intensity. However, Belgium, which has the highest generosity

**Table 8.2** Cases by duration and generosity

| *Country* | *Duration* | *Generosity* |
|---|---|---|
| Austria | 36 | 67.36 |
| Belgium | Unlimited | 70.76 |
| Finland | 71 | 70.45 |
| France | 60.5 | 66.51 |
| Germany | 65 | 63.38 |
| Greece | 36.5 | 31.83 |
| Italy | 30 | 27.08 |
| Norway | 104 | 68.41 |
| Spain | 60.5 | 61.10 |
| UK | 26 | 63.60 |

and longest duration, is not in the low job search set, casting doubt on the hypothesis.

In contrast, the UK has high accessibility and high job search, with both low generosity and short duration. The short duration is mitigated by the fact that the contributory unemployment benefit in the UK (Job seekers' Allowance) is paid at the same flat rate as the social assistance, which is a means-tested version. Germany, with low generosity (although only just below the median cut off point) and long duration, with low job search, contradicts the hypothesis. Based on the case study analysis, the overall conclusion is that duration and generosity of unemployment benefits have no mediating effect on job search behaviour at the aggregate level.

### *Summary of the Case Studies*

The case studies examined two potential causal mechanisms that may help to explain the presence of high or low job search amongst the cases. They found the presence of a 'work first' focus on the administration of unemployment benefits in both Germany and UK. However, they led to different outcomes, suggesting that a work first approach may still not be sufficient for the presence of high job search, but may require additional factors, including the presence of onerous job search requirements. In contrast, the presence of a 'human capital' approach to the administration may be sufficient for the presence of low job search. The case studies also examined the potential causal mechanisms of benefit duration and generosity, however, no relationships were identified between these and high or low job search.

The lack of clear necessity or sufficiency relationships suggests that welfare regimes operate as complex institutional ecosystems rather than as collections of discrete incentive mechanisms. This complexity may stem from how different welfare mechanisms interact in ways not captured by examining individual conditions. The divergence between welfare administration model, 'work first' versus 'human capital' approaches, illustrates this complexity. Whilst conventional theory might predict uniformly higher job search intensity under work first regimes, the analysis shows that administrative philosophy alone does not determine outcomes. The UK and Germany both employ work first approaches yet produce markedly different job search patterns, suggesting that implementation details significantly mediate policy effects. The case studies reveal important differences in how unemployed people experience ostensibly similar policy frameworks. In Germany, for instance, integration contracts formally require intensive job seeking, yet unlike the UK, they lack specific time requirements or stringent verification processes. These qualitative differences in implementation may significantly influence how individuals allocate their time and effort. The stark contrast between formal requirements and observed behaviour is particularly evident in the UK, where despite mandates to treat job search as a full-time commitment, very few unemployed individuals report anything approaching this level of activity. This suggests that individuals may respond to the 'perceived' rather than formal requirements of welfare systems, adapting their behaviour based on how policies are actually implemented rather than how they are designed.

### *Reconsidering Work Incentives in Welfare Regimes*

These findings have implications for basic income design. Both critics and proponents have often based their arguments on relatively straightforward assumptions about how specific welfare mechanisms influence behaviour. The analysis presented in this book suggests a more nuanced reality where institutional context may determine outcomes more than policy design itself.

For basic income implementation, this suggests that identical programmes might produce substantially different behavioural responses depending on the welfare system they replace, combined with the broader institutional environment. A basic income introduced in a Nordic context might function very differently from one implemented in a liberal welfare regime with minimal employment support services.

The findings challenge the notions that unconditionality would reduce work motivation and low PTR would increase motivation. The lack of clear relationship between conditionality, PTRs and job search intensity suggests that other aspects of welfare design and implementation may be more influential. Basic income might therefore need to be accompanied by complementary institutional structures rather than being viewed as a standalone solution.

The contradictions between theory and empirical findings raise important methodological questions. Whilst our QCA approach reveals configurational complexity that would escape linear models, it may still not capture all relevant aspects of welfare systems and their implementation. Cross sectional analysis provides a valuable snapshot but cannot fully account for dynamic processes or long term adaptations within welfare regimes. Future research might benefit from combining QCA with longitudinal approaches to better understand how behaviours evolve as individuals and institutions adapt to changing welfare arrangements.

Another consideration is whether traditional measures of job search intensity fully capture meaningful labour market engagement. Time spent in formal job search activities may not reflect the quality or effectiveness of search strategies. A basic income might, for instance, enable more selective but ultimately more productive job seeking that isn't captured in raw intensity measures.

The findings necessitate theoretical reconsideration of how welfare regimes influence labour market behaviour. Rather than assuming direct relationships between specific mechanisms and behavioural outcomes, the framework used in this book emphasises the importance of institutional contexts.

The contradictions between theoretical expectations and empirical findings in the analysis reveal the limitations of conventional approaches to understanding welfare incentives. Rather than viewing basic income through the lens of isolated mechanisms, it should be conceptualised as an intervention in complex institutional ecosystems where outcomes emerge from the interaction of formal policies, implementation practices, cultural contexts, and individual responses. This more nuanced understanding offers a stronger foundation for designing basic income policies that can achieve their intended effects across diverse welfare contexts.

The next chapter addresses the question of what these findings might mean for basic income and its implementation. Chapter eight applies the empirical results to ongoing basic income debate, examining how the complex relationships between welfare design and job search behaviour could inform potential policy outcomes. It contrasts theoretical expectations with the empirical findings here and employs counterfactual analysis to explore how basic income might function in contrasting welfare regimes, specifically Finland and the UK. Rather than assuming basic income would produce uniform effects across contexts, it examines how its defining principles might influence job search behaviour within different institutional settings.

## References


Allan, J. P., & Scruggs, L. (2004). Political partisanship and welfare state reform in advanced industrial societies. *American Journal of Political Science, 48*(3), 496–512. https://doi.org/10.1111/j.0092-5853.2004.00083.x

Boland, T. (2016). Seeking a role: Disciplining jobseekers as actors in the labour market. *Work, Employment and Society, 30*(2), 334–351. https://doi.org/10.1177/0950017015594097

Card, D., & Levine, P. B. (2000). Extended benefits and the duration of UI spells: Evidence from the New Jersey extended benefit program. *Journal of Public Economics, 78*(1–2), 107–138.

Chetty, R. (2008). Moral hazard versus liquidity and optimal unemployment insurance. *Journal of Political Economy, 116*(2), 173–234. https://doi.org/10.1086/588585

Clasen, J., & Clegg, D. (2011). Unemployment protection and labour market change in Europe: Towards 'triple integration. In *Regulating the risk of unemployment. National adaptations to post-industrial labour markets in Europe*, 1 (p. 13).

Corsini, L. (2013). *A comparative analysis on the relationship between benefits generosity, search requirements and unemployment duration*. Universita'degli Studi di Firenze, Dipartimento di Scienze per l'Economia e .... Retrieved April 22, 2024, from https://www.disei.unifi.it/upload/sub/pubblicazioni/repec/pdf/wp21_2013.pdf

CPAG. (2015). *Welfare benefits and tax credits handbook*. Child Poverty Action Group.

Daguerre, A., & Etherington, D. (2009). *Active labour market policies in international context: What works best? Lessons for the UK*. Crown Copyright. Retrieved April 22, 2024, from https://research.brighton.ac.uk/en/publications/active-labour-market-policies-in-international-context-what-works

Dingeldey, I. (2011). Fragmented governance continued: The German Case. In R. Van Berkel, W. De Graaf, & T. Sirovátka (Eds.), *The governance of active welfare states in Europe* (pp. 62–84). Palgrave Macmillan UK. https://doi.org/10.1057/9780230306714_4

Dolton, P., & O'Neill, D. (2002). The long-run effects of unemployment monitoring and work-search programs: Experimental evidence from the United Kingdom. *Journal of Labor Economics, 20*(2), 381–403. https://doi.org/10.1086/338686

Esping-Andersen, G. (1990). *The three worlds of welfare capitalism*. Princeton University Press. Retrieved March 27, 2024, from https://books.google.com/books?hl=en&lr=&id=ERCnDwAAQBAJ&oi=fnd&pg=PR8&dq=three+worlds+of+welfare+capitalism&ots=0EcmiFe_Uv&sig=2lh58kMmmKErWBF7jdUVGplpIjY

Filiz, E. S. (2017). The effect of unemployment insurance generosity on unemployment duration and labor market transitions. *Labour, 31*(4), 369–393. https://doi.org/10.1111/labr.12104

Gorter, C., & Kalb, G. R. (1996). Estimating the effect of counseling and monitoring the unemployed using a job search model. *Journal of Human Resources, 31*, 590–610.

Johnson, T. R., & Klepinger, D. H. (1994). Experimental evidence on unemployment insurance work-search policies. *Journal of Human Resources, 29*, 695–717.

Karjalainen, V., & Saikku, P. (2011). Governance of integrated activation policy in Finland. In R. Van Berkel, W. De Graaf, & T. Sirovátka (Eds.), *The governance of active welfare states in Europe* (pp. 216–236). Palgrave Macmillan UK. https://doi.org/10.1057/9780230306714_11

Katz, L. F., & Meyer, B. D. (1990). The impact of the potential duration of unemployment benefits on the duration of unemployment. *Journal of Public Economics, 41*(1), 45–72.

Korpi, W., & Palme, J. (2003). New politics and class politics in the context of austerity and globalization: Welfare state regress in 18 countries, 1975–95. *American Political Science Review, 97*(3), 425–446.

Lalive, R., Van Ours, J., & Zweimüller, J. (2006). How changes in financial incentives affect the duration of unemployment. *The Review of Economic Studies, 73*(4), 1009–1038.

Le Barbanchon, T. (2013). The effect of the generosity of unemployment benefits on the duration of unemployment and match quality. *Notes IPP* [Preprint], (5). Retrieved April 22, 2024, from https://shs.hal.science/hal shs-02527071/

Levy, J.D. (2004). Activation through thick and thin: Progressive approaches to labour market activation. In *Social policy review 16* (pp. 187–208). Policy Press. Retrieved April 22, 2024, from https://bristoluniversitypressdigital.com/display/book/9781847425973/ch010.xml

Lichter, A. (2016). *Benefit duration and job search effort: Evidence from a natural experiment*. Retrieved January 25, 2024, from https://papers.ssrn.com/sol3/papers.cfm?abstract_id=2849749

Mahoney, J. (2008). Toward a unified theory of causality. *Comparative Political Studies, 41*(4–5), 412–436. https://doi.org/10.1177/0010414007313115

Marie, O., & Castello, J. V. (2012). Measuring the (income) effect of disability insurance generosity on labour market participation. *Journal of Public Economics, 96*(1–2), 198–210.

McVicar, D. (2008). Job search monitoring intensity, unemployment exit and job entry: Quasi-experimental evidence from the UK. *Labour Economics, 15*(6), 1451–1468.

Minas, R. (2014). One-stop shops: Increasing employability and overcoming welfare state fragmentation? *International Journal of Social Welfare*. https://doi.org/10.1111/ijsw.12090

Minogue, R. (2018). Five problems with basic income. *Third Way*. https://www.thirdway.org/memo/five-problems-with-universal-basic-income. Accessed on 20 April 2024.

Peck, J., & Theodore, N. (2000). Commentary. 'Work first': workfare and the regulation of contingent labour markets. *Cambridge Journal of Economics, 24*(1), 119–138.

Ragin, C. C. (2014). *The comparative method: Moving beyond qualitative and quantitative strategies*. Univ of California Press. Retrieved March 27, 2024, from https://books.google.com/books?hl=en&lr=&id=2akwDwAAQBAJ&oi=fnd&pg=PR7&dq=Ragin,+C.+C.+(1987).+The+comparative+method+:+moving+beyond+qualitative+and++quantitative+strategies.+Berkeley,+CA.+%3B+London:+University+of+California+Press&ots=vfS8Ik3Wu2&sig=G-THxGeOTr8vk173Ts7YtI7RzRI

Schmieder, J. F., von Wachter, T., & Bender, S. (2012). The long-term effects of UI extensions on employment. *American Economic Review, 102*(3), 514–519.

Schneider, C. Q. (2008). *The consolidation of democracy: Comparing Europe and Latin America*. Routledge. Retrieved March 27, 2024, from https://api.taylorfrancis.com/content/books/mono/download?identifierName=doi&identifierValue=10.4324/9780203886779&type=googlepdf

Schneider, C. Q., & Rohlfing, I. (2013). Combining QCA and process tracing in set-theoretic multi-method research. *Sociological Methods & Research, 42*(4), 559–597. https://doi.org/10.1177/0049124113481341

Setty, O. (2019). Optimal unemployment insurance with monitoring. *Quantitative Economics, 10*(2), 693–733. https://doi.org/10.3982/QE564

Torry, M. (2018). Some lessons from the recent UK debate about. 19.

Van Ours, J. C., & Vodopivec, M. (2006). How Shortening the potential duration of unemployment benefits affects the duration of unemployment: Evidence from a natural experiment. *Journal of Labor Economics, 24*(2), 351–378. https://doi.org/10.1086/499976

Van Vliet, O., & Caminada, K. (2012). *Unemployment replacement rates dataset among 34 welfare states, 1971–2009: An update, extension and modification of the Scruggs' welfare state entitlements data set*. Retrieved April 22, 2024, from https://papers.ssrn.com/sol3/papers.cfm?abstract_id=1991214

Vodopivec, M., et al. (2015). *The effect of unemployment benefit generosity on unemployment duration: Quasi-experimental evidence from Slovenia*. Retrieved April 22, 2024, from https://papers.ssrn.com/sol3/papers.cfm?abstract_id=2708361

White, J. (2023). *Universal basic income: A pointless trial of a bad idea*. Institute of Economic Affairs.

https://iea.org.uk/universal-basic-income-a-pointless-trial- of-a-bad-idea/. Accessed on 06 March 2024.

Wiggan, J. (2007). Reforming the United Kingdom's public employment and social security agencies. *International Review of Administrative Sciences, 73*(3), 409–424. https://doi.org/10.1177/0020852307081150

CHAPTER 9

# Exploring the Potential Impact of Basic Income on Job Search Behaviours

**Abstract** Chapter nine applies the findings from previous chapters to basic income debates and examines the potential policy implications for basic income implementation. It contrasts the major theoretical debates around basic income and work incentives with the empirical findings in chapter seven. It then uses counterfactual analysis to examine basic income's potential effects across diverse welfare contexts. The findings demonstrate that basic income's effects would not follow straightforward theoretical expectations but would depend on complex interactions within broader institutional arrangements. Through counterfactual analysis, the chapter illustrates how identical basic income implementations may produce different outcomes based on existing welfare regimes. The chapter concludes that basic income should not be conceptualised as incentivising work but rather as enhancing income security within specific institutional contexts that ultimately determine its freedom enhancing potential.

**Keywords** Counterfactual analysis · Institutional context · Finnish welfare model · UK welfare system · Labour market flexibility · Precarious employment · Implementation pathways



S. Watkins, *Basic Income, Work Incentives and Job Search Behaviour*, Exploring the Basic Income Guarantee,
https://doi.org/10.1007/978-3-031-99197-4_9

Chapter eight's fuzzy set qualitative comparative analysis of job search intensity across ten European countries yielded three key findings that challenge conventional wisdom about welfare incentives.

Firstly, no welfare mechanisms, either in isolation or in conjunction with others, proved necessary or sufficient for high job search intensity, undermining arguments that strict conditionality requirements and low participation tax rates incentivise job search activity. Secondly, a specific configuration combining high participation tax rates with high accessibility to unemployment benefits was found to be sufficient for the presence of low job search intensity, demonstrating welfare incentives' configurational and asymmetrical nature. Thirdly, case studies revealed significant qualitative differences in the implementation and administration of welfare mechanisms, specifically behavioural conditionality, which may have significant impact on job search behaviour, and point to the importance of specific contextual factors when examining the potential impact of basic income.

This chapter applies these empirical findings to basic income debates by exploring how complex relationships between welfare design and job search behaviour might inform our understanding of basic income's potential effects across diverse contexts. It examines how it's defining features, unconditionality, universality and non-withdrawable payments, might influence job search activity in different institutional settings.

The chapter is split into three parts. The first analyses how the empirical findings from earlier chapters challenge or support key theoretical claims in basic income debates. The second part develops a framework for understanding how institutional context mediates basic income effects. The third section employs counterfactual analysis to explore how basic income might function in two contrasting welfare contexts, Finland and the UK, both of which represent divergent approaches to welfare benefits for the unemployed.

Chapter eight's findings suggest that basic income's effects would not follow straightforwardly from theoretical expectations. Instead, as this chapter will demonstrate, its impact on job search behaviour likely depends on the complex interaction of multiple mechanisms embedded within broader institutional arrangements and cultural contexts.

## Implications of Empirical Findings for Basic Income theory

This section explores what the findings of the QCA and case studies mean for debates around the potential impact of a basic income on the job search activity of the unemployed. It firstly examines the findings in relation to the empirical and theoretical expectations of each condition, then explores the findings more broadly and what they mean for basic income as a potential form of welfare.

### *Reconsidering Concerns Around Labour Market Participation*

One of the main concerns around basic income is the idea that behavioural conditionality is necessary to maintain or even increase motivations to search for employment. The argument follows that the removal of behavioural conditions would reduce motivation to find employment, undermining labour market participation and increasing periods of unemployment. This fear underpins much of the political consensus around the effectiveness of conditionality that has driven 'activation' policies across Europe over the last three decades (Knotz, 2018). However, the empirical findings of this research challenge these assumptions.

The QCA analysis found that high levels of conditionality were neither necessary nor sufficient for the presence of high job search intensity. The analysis also found that unconditionality was not necessary nor sufficient for the presence of low job search. These findings counter theoretical expectations, aligning with recent basic income experiments in Finland (Kangas et. al., 2021) and Ontario (McDowell & Ferdosi, 2021), both of which found minimal negative effects on labour market participation following the introduction of basic income payments. Findings from the Finnish experiment are particularly instructive, as unemployed benefit recipients who received basic income had similar re-employment levels to those of the control group, who remained subject to existing conditionality within the Finnish welfare system.

The case studies offer further evidence that conditionality operates through mechanisms beyond formal policy design, with each welfare regime administering conditionality in different ways, leading to a range of outcomes. Whilst conditionality retains a 'performative' role in current welfare policies, demonstrating and reinforcing social norms of reciprocity and the notion of deserving welfare it does not appear to be effective in incentivising unemployed people to search for suitable work.

### *Reassessing the Effects of Financial Incentives*

Basic income has been proposed as a solution to the 'unemployment trap', where benefit withdrawal, combined with means-testing creates situations where it is financially unattractive to take on paid work (Torry, 2017). The argument is that, as a non-withdrawable, non means-tested payment basic income would enhance financial incentives to work by reducing the high participation tax rates that characterise many existing welfare regimes relating to unemployment benefits.

However, the findings of this research suggest that increased financial incentives may not be a significant factor in job search behaviour, as low participation tax rates were not found to be necessary or sufficient for the presence of high job search intensity. This finding aligns with evidence from the Finnish basic income experiment, where significant reductions in participation tax rates did not produce corresponding increases in employment outcomes (Verho et al., 2022). The lack of behavioural responses to improved financial incentives suggests that such incentives, whilst making theoretical sense, have little impact in the real world.

In contrast, high participation tax rates, when combined with highly accessible benefits, were sufficient for low job search intensity. This asymmetrical relationship suggests that whilst high financial disincentives may discourage job search activity when paired with accessible benefits, removing these disincentives does not automatically increase job search intensity.

The implications for basic income advocates are significant, as the findings from this research, and from basic income experiments, strongly suggest that basic income should not be conceptualised primarily as a policy which incentivises job search activity. Whilst it would remove certain financial disincentives associated with benefit withdrawal and means-testing, basic income may be better understood in terms of improving income security and reduced poverty than as a mechanism for increasing work motivation.

### *Reevaluating Universality Effects*

Basic income universalism contrasts with the targeted eligibility requirements of most welfare regimes. Critics have argued that universal payments may undermine work motivation, on the basis that easy access to cash benefits removes the immediate financial requirement to work thereby disincentivising job search behaviour.

The findings of this research show that high accessibility to unemployment benefits is not, on its own, sufficient for the presence of low job search intensity. However, high accessibility combined with high participation tax rates was found to be sufficient. The combination of these two disincentives highlights the importance of considering how the universal nature of basic income might interact with other welfare regime characteristics.

Case studies examined the potential roles of benefit duration and generosity as mediating factors influencing job search behaviour. Research has linked both the duration and generosity of unemployment benefits to labour market participation, suggesting that more generous benefits, paid for a longer period, would create a greater disincentive to look for work. Benefit generosity has been linked with longer spells of unemployment (Corsini, 2013; Le Barbanchon, 2013; Vodopivec et al., 2015; Filiz, 2017) and many advocates as well as opponents of basic income agree that basic income, paid at a high enough level, would act as a disincentive to find work. Previous research has shown that the duration of benefit payments has an impact on job search, with increased duration resulting in longer periods of benefit receipt (Card & Levine, 2000; Chetty, 2008; Katz & Meyer, 1990; Lalive et al., 2005; Schmieder et al., 2012; Van Ours & Vodopivec, 2006).However, the case studies that accompanied the QCA analysis found no clear relationship between the two factors and job search intensity. Countries with similar levels of benefit duration and generosity demonstrated varying levels of job search intensity, suggesting that these factors alone do not determine job search behaviour. The findings suggest that concerns about basic income universality leading to reduced work motivation may be misplaced.

### *The Non-Linear Relationship Between Welfare Mechanisms and Behavioural Outcomes*

Perhaps the most important insight gained from the empirical analysis conducted in this book is how welfare regimes act in non-linear, configurational ways to impact on behaviour. Rather than each mechanism having a discrete, predictable effect, the findings suggest that outcomes emerge from complex interactions between welfare characteristics, implementation, and institutional contexts.

Such complexity challenges both critics and advocates of basic income who have based their arguments on relatively straightforward causal assumptions, which generally rely on analysis of causal mechanisms in isolation. It is clear that basic income should be conceptualised, not as a collection of discrete mechanisms with predictable effects, but as an intervention in complex institutional contexts. This perspective argues that basic income schemes, whilst identical in design, may produce significantly different behavioural responses, depending on the welfare regimes they replace and the broader institutional and cultural environments into which they are introduced.

By moving beyond simplistic causal models, the empirical findings point towards a more nuanced framework for understanding basic income, one that acknowledges causal complexity, emphasises institutional context, and recognises the limitations of predicting behavioural responses based on isolated policy mechanisms.

To further explore how complex institutional dynamics might shape basic income outcomes across different welfare contexts, the next section uses counterfactual analysis or thought experiments to explore how basic income might function in two countries with contrasting welfare regimes and levels of job search intensity: Finland and the UK.

## Counterfactual Analysis: Introducing Basic Income in Finland the UK

The use of thought experiments in social science research, particularly in comparative and historical studies, is a useful methodological approach for exploring counterfactual scenarios (Ragin & Sonnett, 2005). An 'instrument of armchair science' (Elsenbroich & Gilbert, 2014: 6), the thought experiment is an important part of scientific advancement. It uses 'what if' reasoning to explore hypothetical situations that do not occur but are imagined for analytical purposes, enabling researchers to examine the causal significance of components within complex systems (Ragin & Sonnett, 2005).

Thought experiments in social research involve the construction of hypothetical scenarios to test the implications of different causal variables, often with one or more significant differences from existing or historical reality. For example, Moore (1993) imaged a scenario where the Confederate States won the US Civil War to explore the conditions necessary for the emergence of democratic political systems. Exploring counterfactual scenarios helps researchers understand cause and effect where large scale social experiments are impractical (Ragin & Sonnett, 2005). This approach is especially helpful when studying basic income, since it doesn't exist in practice, we need to use counterfactual analysis to understand what might happen if it were implemented. This thought experiment focuses on the argument that the impact of basic income is likely to depend on the institutional context into which it is placed (2019a; De Wispelaere & Haagh, 2019; Haagh's, 2011, 2015). State provided services, including other welfare policies in place, are likely to be significant factors in shaping the effects of basic income.

Haagh (2019a) makes the argument is that a more supportive state is likely to give rise to more positive, 'freedom enhancing' effects than contexts with less support in place. In this respect, the Nordic countries are commonly framed as having higher levels of support for their residents, from universal welfare to accessible childcare. In contrast, the UK is viewed as providing a far less supportive environment, with strict conditionality applied to meagre welfare arrangements and a reliance on the private sector for many provisions, including childcare.

Given these two contrasting institutional contexts, this part uses counterfactual analysis to examine the potential effects of basic income on job search activity amongst unemployed people. It also broadens out to examine the potential effects on labour market participation and labour markets themselves. Each country starts from a different point, in terms of job search intensity amongst the unemployed, with high job search intensity in the UK and low job search intensity in Finland. The purpose of this thought experiment is to assess how these may change, or not, following the introduction of a basic income.

In undertaking these thought experiments, the following assumptions are made:

- A 'modest' basic income is introduced, paid around or just below existing social assistance benefit levels in each country.
- Basic income replaces existing flat rate unemployment/social assistance payments only, leaving all other benefits in place.
- There are no other immediate changes to the existing institutional arrangements, such as the role of the job centre or employment office, although it is assumed that these may change over time.

### *Basic Income in Finland: Subtle Shifts Rather Than Radical Reform*

Finland's welfare regime is characterised as conditional, accessible, and with high participation tax rates. It is also in the low job search intensity set. In the QCA analysis in chapter eight the combination of accessible benefits and high participation tax rates was found to be sufficient for the presence of low job search intensity. The case studies further identified that Finland has generous unemployment benefits which are paid for a long period of time, and although a member of the conditional set, the administration of conditionality is characterised by a 'human capital' approach, with job seekers offered a range of personalised services and activities, including education and practical training for developing everyday life skills (Karjalainen & Saikku, 2011).

A basic income in Finland would remove conditionality, extend accessibility, and reduce participation tax rates. These represent potentially significant changes to the existing system, with knock on effects for job search behaviour. The assessment of the potential impact on job search activity is shaped by the findings from previous chapters in this book and the Finnish basic income experiment conducted between 2016 and 2018, which provides valuable empirical insights for the counterfactual analysis.

The QCA analysis in the previous chapter identified the combination of high accessibility and high participation tax rates as sufficient for the presence of low job search. Finland combines both conditions as well as the outcome. The introduction of basic income would remove high participation tax rates, therefore removing a financial disincentive to find work. However, the QCA analysis found no evidence to suggest that low participation tax rates lead to increased levels of job search activity. This finding supports those made by the Finnish basic income experiment which found that reducing participation tax rates did not increase re-employment rates amongst the unemployed participants.

Given that job search activity in Finland starts at a low base, it would be unlikely to decrease further, as the removal of conditionality in the Finnish experiment did not result in lower re-employment levels, but it may not increase either. The remaining institutional factors still in place, particularly the 'human capital' approach of the administration of benefits, may function to limit increases in job search activity. The introduction of a basic income may therefore have only marginal effects on job search activity in Finland.

The purpose of the Finnish basic income experiment was to remove financial disincentives and bureaucratic barriers to work amongst the unemployed, reducing high marginal tax rates on moving from unemployment to work and removing the requirement to report job search activities to the employment office (De Wispelaere et al., 2019). However, the overall impact on the number of days worked by recipients was minimal. Whilst the effects on aggregate job search intensity may not change significantly in the short term, there are several potential changes over the longer term, which are worth considering.

Although the overall working hours were not significantly different between basic income recipients and the control group, basic income recipients showed an increased tendency towards part-time employment compared to the control group. This may have been driven, at least in part, by the receipt of the basic income, enabling people to take on part-time rather than full-time work. This suggests that a more flexible labour market may appear over time, with an increase in part-time positions. However, it is important to note that survey data suggested that most of those in part-time work would rather be working full-time. Whilst basic income enabled people to work part-time, it was not necessarily as a lifestyle choice (Kangas et al., 2021).

The number of unemployed moving back into part-time work rather than full-time work may increase over time. This may have knock on effects for the labour market, which may change over time to increase the proportion of jobs that are part-time rather than full-time. This, in turn, may then have the effect of increasing the number of unemployed people who move back into work, but into part-time jobs. Whilst this may be beneficial for some who value the flexibility of part-time work, it may not be suitable for many who would prefer full-time work, as survey data from the Finnish experiment found—most of those in part-time work had a preference for full-time work (Kangas & Ylikännö, 2023). This may lead to frustration with the labour market, as people want full-time work, but cannot access it.

In contrast, the basic income may enable people to refuse part-time work and continue searching for more appropriate work. This may be the case for those with high levels of confidence about finding work in the coming year. Basic income enables them to continue job search activities in the knowledge that the basic income will not be withdrawn due to behavioural conditions or the expiration of entitlement, providing them with more financial security, whilst they continue to look for a job. This is a logical extension of Haagh's (2019) interpretation of the Finnish results demonstrating the freedom enhancing potential of basic income.

The Finnish experiment also found the continued use of employment services and ALMP amongst unemployed recipients, despite the attachment of behavioural conditions for doing so. This finding suggests that basic income recipients did not object to the conditionality of the employment service and/or they valued these services above and beyond any objections they had to being subjected to behavioural conditions (Hiilamo, 2022). This suggests that the presence or absence of conditionality is not a substantive element in people's decision making around job search activity, particularly if it is administered from a 'human capital' approach. The introduction of basic income in Finland is not therefore likely to reduce search activity.

Finally, basic income increased levels of confidence about becoming employed over the coming year amongst recipients, suggesting a significant empowering effect (Kangas et al., 2021). Although increased confidence in becoming employed in the next year may have no actual bearing on the overall probability of becoming employed, it does at least suggest a reason for higher levels of motivation to look for work, assuming that unemployed people who are confident of getting a job are more likely to continue job search activities than those who do not feel confident about their employment prospects.

This counterfactual analysis suggests that a basic income in Finland is likely to produce subtle shifts in existing patterns rather than radical changes in behaviour. The 'human capital' approach would continue to provide support and structure to those looking for work, with basic income primarily enhancing flexibility and financial security within this institutional context.

### *Basic Income in the UK: Reinforcing Precarious Work*

The UK welfare regime is characterised by high accessibility and low participation tax rates but differs mostly from the Finnish model through its exceptionally high levels of conditionality, combined with a 'work first' approach to the administration of benefits. The UK starts from a position of high job search intensity amongst the unemployed.

The introduction of basic income in the UK would therefore dramatically alter the UK welfare regime. Whilst benefits are already accessible with low participation tax rates, basic income would remove its defining characteristic of high conditionality, with potentially more significant effects on job search activity and the labour market in the UK than we might see in Finland.

The analysis in chapter eight suggests that, although high conditionality alone is not sufficient for the presence of high job search, underlying mechanisms combining very high job search requirements, including a 'work first' emphasis on the administration of benefits and monitoring may be contributory factors leading to high job search intensity. Although basic income would remove behavioural conditions, monitoring, and sanctions, its impact on the 'work first' emphasis of benefit administration is harder to judge.

The removal of job search requirements means that unemployed people would no longer be required to spend up to 35 hours a week in job search activities. The removal of this requirement may lead to a reduction in job search activities as people feel less compelled to undertake such activities. However, as the time use data showed, only 1% of unemployed people spent more than four hours in job search activities on a given day, with the majority spending less than an hour on it. This suggests that the 35 hour rule is not adhered to, and its removal may not therefore generate a significant changes in behaviour.

The removal of monitoring requirements may lead to a dissipation of the 'work first' emphasis of the administration. Whilst Job centres may still focus on getting people into the first work that becomes available, they would lose the punitive powers to impose sanctions on those who refused. The removal of both strict monitoring and the threat of sanctions may result in fewer people using the job centre and just looking for themselves. Job centres would then either presumably close or be re-purposed to be more supportive of training and education, rather than focusing on getting people back into the first job available (assuming also that they function as administrators of other benefits also—they would still be required). A change in the culture and or nature of Job centres may therefore occur, but over a more extended period.

Based on the removal of these factors, there may be a decrease in job search activity if we assume that conditionality is responsible for high job search, although the findings presented in chapter 7 do not support this assumption. Instead, there may be two reactions. Basic income may result in people being able to take more time to find a job that is suitable for them (assuming again that such jobs exist and are available). This may not result in an overall decrease in job search activity, and may increase it overall, as people spend longer and look with more purpose, rather than taking on any work, as they are currently obliged to do. Although the increase would be measured over a potentially longer period (meaning that if the method for measuring job search used in this book were used to measure job search activity in the UK following the introduction of a basic income—we might see a decrease in job search activity if, for example, people searched only 1 day a week instead of 2).

Alternatively, the unemployed may use basic income to take up part-time or low wage work, to boost their income, in the absence of better paid or more secure work. Within this context, it may be that those at the lower income scale could use the precarious labour market to their advantage by using basic income as a 'job subsidy' to take on part-time, or short term work that they would not be able to without the additional income that the basic income gives them. In the short term, it may therefore be that, absent a reaction to the removal of strict conditionality and monitoring, which the research does not support, the introduction of a basic income in the UK would not see a dramatic reduction in job search amongst unemployed people in the UK.

The UK's already flexible labour market might experience further segmentation. For some workers, basic income could provide sufficient security to reject poor wages or working conditions, potentially improving wages and conditions in certain sectors. For others, particularly those with limited bargaining power, basic income may actually reinforce dependence on precarious work by making it financially sustainable enough to accept.

Unlike in Finland, where basic income may enhance flexibility within a supportive institutional framework based around a 'human capital' approach, weaker institutional protections in the UK may lead to basic income subsidising the expansion of low paid work. Rather than empowering those on low pay to reject poor conditions, basic income might normalise low paid, insecure work for a significant portion of the workforce.

The impact of basic income in the UK would remain heavily constrained by existing institutional configurations that currently maintain high job search activity. Without complementary reforms to employment protection, education and training, as well as labour market regulation, basic income alone would be unlikely to fundamentally transform the UK's employment landscape. The limited supportive services would continue to shape outcomes, even with the removal of conditionality. Unlike Finland's 'human capital' approach, which might complement basic income to enhance freedom and flexibility, the UK's institutional context might limit basic income's transformative potential.

In summary, basic income in the UK context might function more as a subsidy for a flexible, precarious labour market than as a tool for genuine liberation and security. Without the supporting institutional framework found in Nordic countries, basic income risks becoming absorbed into and potentially reinforcing existing patterns of labour market inequality, rather than transforming them.

## Institutional Contexts Matter: How Welfare Regimes Shape Basic Income Outcomes

The thought experiments support the arguments made by Haagh (2019), that basic income is not necessarily a freedom enhancing policy but is dependent on the institutional arrangements that surround it. Although the options available to hypothetical basic income recipients in Finland and the UK are the same, i.e. remain unemployed (don't look for a job), get a part-time job to supplement basic income (either out of choice or necessity), or keep looking for the most suitable job (assumed to be for the majority of people—full-time), the impact of basic income in both countries would be constrained by the institutional configurations that exist in each to, firstly keep job search activity in Finland low and secondly keep job search activity in the UK high.

This may change over time, as the culture of administration in the UK may become less focused on a 'work first' approach, or if the proportion of part-time work in Finland begins to increase, we may see more of a convergence in behaviours. Particularly if sections of the job market become ever more flexible, as the proportion of part-time work increase. This may produce more of a 'flexicurity' system in both countries, characterised by very flexible labour markets with low levels of worker protection, but high levels of compensatory social protection (Bekker & Mailand, 2019). The combination of flexible labour markets and basic income provision of income floor could attract unemployed people back into the labour market, who would otherwise not re-engage. However, the development of a 'flexicurity' system in the UK is less likely, given the current low levels of social protection afforded to people. Instead, the diffusion of low paid, insecure work may in fact continue under a basic income. Rather than helping the 'precariat', by providing them with a means of saying no to low paid, insecure work, the institutional arrangements in the UK may result in the reinforcement of such work for a significant proportion of the workforce, acting as the 'exit trap' warned of by Birnbaum and De Wispelaere (2021), where people on low incomes are unable to escape from poorly paid, part-time work.

Increased flexibility in labour demand is based on making safe full-time jobs less common, which leads to more unstable jobs (Kalleberg, 2018). Some people might like this kind of flexicurity plan, but it's still not clear how a modest basic income impacts on the bargaining power for those on low incomes. It may be that the degree of flexibility within existing labour markets would create divergent paths, with more rigid labour markets having the effect of driving up reservation wages, and more flexible job markets becoming even more prevalent. To understand this better, we need more evidence on the labour demand as well as supply response.

This thought experiment suggests potential outcomes, based on existing theoretical and empirical knowledge, and is but one of many routes that may be taken should a basic income be introduced. What it does highlight is that the effects of a basic income would be shaped by the institutional context into which it is placed.

Overall, this book argues that basic income would have little overall effect on existing job search activity levels amongst the unemployed at the aggregate level across European countries, particularly over the short term.

The book finds that the interaction between welfare mechanisms of conditionality, participation tax and accessibility have an asymmetrical impact on the job search behaviour of the unemployed. Whilst there appear to be no conditions or configurations of conditions that lead to high job search, high participation tax rates combined with high accessibility may be sufficient for the presence of low job search.

Participation tax rates have been used to illustrate the financial incentive of a basic income to work. However, the book is supportive of evidence from the Finnish basic income experiment that lower participation tax rates are not an incentive to find work (Verho et al., 2022). Whilst high levels of participation tax rates appear to work in conjunction with high accessibility to unemployment benefits to be sufficient for the presence of low job search, low tax rates are not sufficient for the presence of high job search. Low participation tax rates do not therefore appear to be an incentive to find work. Removing conditionality was also found not to have an incentive effect, either in experimental data or in this book.

Basic income is not therefore an inherently incentivising policy. There may be other factors, such as being paid individually, which may impact on incentives, particularly compared to benefits that are based on households rather than individuals but changing these two mechanisms does not appear to have much of an impact on job search behaviour.

The book demonstrates that welfare regimes that are more akin to a basic income do not inherently produce either high or low levels of job search intensity. Additional contextual factors are therefore more important than the lack of conditionality, low participation tax rates, and high levels of accessibility in determining job search activity amongst the unemployed.

The concluding chapter synthesises the journey from theoretical concepts to empirical analysis of basic income principles. It brings together key insights about how institutional contexts mediate welfare effects, challenges assumptions about work incentives, and highlights the interplay between welfare design and administration. It addresses limitations of the current research, outlines promising directions for future inquiry, and offers practical policy implications. This final chapter moves beyond detailed analysis to broader reflections on translating basic income theory into effective implementation, informing both research and policy development.

## References

Bekker, S., & Mailand, M. (2019). The European flexicurity concept and the Dutch and Danish flexicurity models: How have they managed the Great Recession? *Social Policy & Administration*, *53*(1), 142–155. https://doi.org/10.1111/spol.12441

Birnbaum, S., & De Wispelaere, J. (2021). Exit strategy or exit trap? Basic income and the 'power to say no' in the age of precarious employment. *Socio-Economic Review, 19*(3), 909–927.

Card, D., & Levine, P. B. (2000). Extended benefits and the duration of UI spells: Evidence from the New Jersey extended benefit program. *Journal of Public Economics, 78*(1–2), 107–138.

Chetty, R. (2008). Moral Hazard versus Liquidity and Optimal Unemployment Insurance. *Journal of Political Economy, 116*(2), 173–234. https://doi.org/10.1086/588585

Corsini, L. (2013) *A comparative analysis on the relationship between benefits generosity, search requirements and unemployment duration*. Universita'degli Studi di Firenze, Dipartimento di Scienze per l'Economia e.... Retrieved April 22, 2024, from https://www.disei.unifi.it/upload/sub/pubblicazioni/repec/pdf/wp21_2013.pdf

De Wispelaere, J., & Haagh, L. (2019). Introduction: Basic income in European welfare states: Opportunities and constraints. *Social Policy and Society, 18*(2), 237–242.

De Wispelaere, J., Halmetoja, A., & Pulkka, V.-V. (2019). The Finnish basic income experiment: A primer. In M. Torry (Ed.), *The Palgrave international handbook of basic income* (pp. 389–406). Springer International Publishing (Exploring the Basic Income Guarantee). https://doi.org/10.1007/978-3-030-23614-4_20

Elsenbroich, C., & Gilbert, N. (2014). Modelling norms. In C. Elsenbroich & N. Gilbert (Eds.), *Modelling norms* (pp. 143–149). Springer Netherlands. https://doi.org/10.1007/978-94-007-7052-2_10

Filiz, E. S. (2017). The effect of unemployment insurance generosity on unemployment duration and labor market transitions. *Labour, 31*(4), 369–393. https://doi.org/10.1111/labr.12104

Haagh, L. (2011). Basic income, social democracy and control over time. *Policy & Politics, 39*(1), 43–66.

Haagh, L. (2015). Alternative social states and the basic income debate: Institutions, inequality and human development. *Basic Income Studies*. https://doi.org/10.1515/bis-2015-0002

Haagh, L. (2019). The Philosophy and Political Economy of Basic Income Revisited. In M. Torry (Ed.), *The Palgrave International Handbook of Basic Income* (pp. 253–299). Springer International Publishing (Exploring the Basic Income Guarantee). https://doi.org/10.1007/978-3-030-23614-4_14

Hiilamo, H. (2022). Lessons from basic income experiments. In *Participation income* (pp. 51–82). Edward Elgar Publishing. Retrieved January 27, 2024, from https://www.elgaronline.com/monochap-oa/book/9781800880801/book-part-9781800880801-12.xml

Kalleberg, A. L. (2018). *Precarious lives: Job insecurity and well-being in rich democracies*. Wiley.

Kangas, O., et al. (2021). *Experimenting with unconditional basic income: Lessons from the Finnish BI experiment 2017–2018*. Edward Elgar Publishing. Retrieved February 7, 2024, from https://books.google.com/books?hl=en&lr=&id=d3g8EAAAQBAJ&oi=fnd&pg=PR1&dq=Experimenting+with+Unconditional+Basic+Income:+Lessons+from+the+Finnish+BI+...&ots=TOiHW1qqm5&sig=V_cSv1zIVC4jCNSNQxqho7yx8vQ

Kangas, O., & Ylikännö, M. (2023). Basic income and the status of women in an established gender-equal welfare state: Results from the Finnish basic income experiment. *International Journal of Environmental Research and Public Health, 20*(3), 1733.

Karjalainen, V., & Saikku, P. (2011). Governance of integrated activation policy in Finland. In R. Van Berkel, W. De Graaf, & T. Sirovátka (Eds.), *The governance of active welfare states in Europe* (pp. 216–236). Palgrave Macmillan UK. https://doi.org/10.1057/9780230306714_11

Katz, L. F., & Meyer, B. D. (1990). The impact of the potential duration of unemployment benefits on the duration of unemployment. *Journal of Public Economics, 41*(1), 45–72.

Knotz, C. M. (2018). A rising workfare state? Unemployment benefit conditionality in 21 OECD countries, 1980–2012. *Journal of International and Comparative Social Policy, 34*(2), 91–108.

Lalive, R., Van Ours, J. C., & Zweimüller, J. (2005). The effect of benefit sanctions on the duration of unemployment. *Journal of the European Economic Association, 3*(6), 1386–1417.

Le Barbanchon, T. (2013). The effect of the generosity of unemployment benefits on the duration of unemployment and match quality. *Notes IPP* [Preprint], (5). Retrieved April 22, 2024, from https://shs.hal.science/halshs-02527071/

McDowell, T., & Ferdosi, M. (2021). The Impacts of the Ontario Basic Income Pilot: A Comparative Analysis of the Findings from the Hamilton Region. *Basic Income Studies, 16*(2), 209–256. https://doi.org/10.1515/bis-2020-0034

Moore, B. (1993). *Social origins of dictatorship and democracy: Lord and peasant in the making of the modern* world (Vol. 268). Beacon Press.

Ragin, C. C., & Sonnett, J. (2005). Between complexity and parsimony: limited diversity, counterfactual cases, and comparative analysis. In S. Kropp, & M. Minkenberg (Eds.), *Vergleichen in der Politikwissenschaft* (pp. 180–197). VS Verlag für Sozialwissenschaften. https://doi.org/10.1007/978-3-322-80441-9_9

Schmieder, J. F., von Wachter, T., & Bender, S. (2012). The long-term effects of UI extensions on employment. *American Economic Review, 102*(3), 514–519.

Torry, M. (2017). *A variety of indicators evaluated for two implementation methods for a Citizen's Basic Income*. EUROMOD Working Paper. https://www.econstor.eu/handle/10419/197610

Van Ours, J. C., & Vodopivec, M. (2006). How shortening the potential duration of unemployment benefits affects the duration of unemployment: Evidence from a natural experiment. *Journal of Labor Economics, 24*(2), 351–378. https://doi.org/10.1086/499976

Verho, J., Hämäläinen, K., & Kanninen, O. (2022). Removing Welfare Traps: Employment Responses in the Finnish Basic Income Experiment. *American Economic Journal: Economic Policy, 14*(1), 501–522. https://doi.org/10.1257/pol.20200143

Vodopivec, M., et al. (2015). The effect of unemployment benefit generosity on unemployment duration: quasi-experimental evidence from Slovenia. Retrieved April 22, 2024, from https://papers.ssrn.com/sol3/papers.cfm?abstract_id=2708361

CHAPTER 10

# From Theory to Practice: Lessons Learned and Future Directions in Basic Income Research

**Abstract** This concluding chapter recounts the book's journey from theoretical concepts to empirical analysis. It distils the key insights from the research, addresses methodological limitations, and outlines future research directions. It then provides guidance for context contingent implementation strategies, complementary policy frameworks, and transitional pathways towards basic income. The chapter concludes by reflecting on basic income's potential to enhance developmental freedom, particularly the potential for basic income to facilitate meaningful life choices aligned with personal values rather than immediate economic necessities, when implemented within supportive institutional contexts.

**Keywords** Institutional mediation · Policy implications · Research limitations · Implementation strategies · Developmental freedom · Future research · Income security

This concluding chapter traces the book's journey from theoretical concepts to empirical analysis of basic income principles, highlighting key insights for both research and policy development. The investigation has traversed multiple analytical phases, from the defining principles of basic income in Chapter One, through examining experimental evidence



S. Watkins, *Basic Income, Work Incentives and Job Search Behaviour*, Exploring the Basic Income Guarantee,
https://doi.org/10.1007/978-3-031-99197-4_10

in Chapter Two, to developing an innovative methodological framework in Chapters Three through Six that bridges theory and practice.

The book began by establishing the conceptual foundation, identifying how unconditionality, universalism, and non-withdrawal of benefits might theoretically impact job search behaviour. This framework guided subsequent analysis of empirical evidence from basic income experiments worldwide, revealing important patterns in labour market effects whilst highlighting the methodological limitations of purely experimental approaches.

The analytical core of the research employed Qualitative Comparative Analysis (QCA) to measure how closely various European welfare regimes approximate basic income principles and mapped job search intensity across these same welfare regimes. This approach enabled examination of welfare mechanisms in practice and their effects on behaviour, revealing complex, configurational relationships that challenge conventional wisdom about work incentives. Rather than finding simple, linear relationships between policy features and behavioural outcomes, the analysis identified intricate patterns of causality that vary across institutional contexts.

The counterfactual analysis then demonstrated how identical basic income schemes might function differently in contrasting welfare contexts, emphasising why implementation strategies must be tailored to specific institutional arrangements. Throughout this journey, the research has moved beyond abstract debates about whether basic income 'works' towards a more nuanced understanding of how it might work in specific contexts.

The findings challenge prevailing assumptions about work incentives whilst emphasising the critical importance of institutional context in shaping basic income outcomes. This conclusion synthesises these insights, addresses limitations of the current research, outlines promising directions for future inquiry, and offers practical implications for policymakers considering basic income implementation. By grounding predictions in evidence rather than assumptions, this chapter aims to inform both the academic discourse and policy development process, providing a foundation for more realistic expectations and more effective implementation strategies.

## Key Insights and Their Significance

The analysis generated several important insights that challenge prevailing assumptions about basic income and work incentives. Perhaps the most important finding is that institutional context profoundly mediates welfare effects. The same basic income principles produced markedly different outcomes across welfare regimes, suggesting that identical basic income programmes would likely yield different results depending on the institutional contexts into which they are introduced. This finding undermines absolutist claims about basic income's effects, both positive and negative, and highlights the importance of context. Welfare states are not simply collections of individual policies but are complex institutional ecosystems where outcomes emerge from interactions between multiple mechanisms, administrative practices, and cultural norms surrounding work and welfare.

The research finds that behavioural conditionality does not automatically increase job search intensity. Despite the political consensus around activation policies and increased conditionality (Andersen & Larsen, 2024), the research found no evidence that high conditionality was either necessary or sufficient for high job search intensity. This finding aligns with evidence from basic income experiments showing limited behavioural responses to the removal of conditionality (Widerquist, 2005, 2019a; Kangas et al., 2021; McDowell & Ferdosi, 2021; Riutort et al., 2023; Mathur et al., 2025). These findings support a growing literature which questions the efficacy and morality of the use of behavioural conditions in the administration of welfare benefits (Ball et al., 2019; Jones et al., 2024; Reeves & Loopstra, 2017; Watts & Fitzpatrick, 2018).

Financial incentives operate in complex, asymmetrical ways. Whilst the combination of high participation tax rates and high accessibility was sufficient for low job search intensity, the antithesis, low participation tax rates, did not produce high job search intensity. This asymmetry suggests that whilst certain combinations of disincentives may discourage work effort, their removal does not automatically create incentives. This challenges both critics who fear work disincentives from basic income and advocates who claim it would enhance work incentives through reduced marginal tax rates. The findings support evidence from the Finnish basic income experiment that reducing participation tax rates does not act as an incentive to enter the work force (Verho et al., 2022).

Welfare effects emerge from configurations rather than isolated mechanisms. Individual policy features rarely produce outcomes in isolation; instead, effects emerge from complex interactions between multiple mechanisms. This configurational causality helps explain why debates focused on single mechanisms (like conditionality or participation tax rates) often yield contradictory conclusions, as they fail to capture how these mechanisms interact within specific institutional contexts (Ragin, 2004).

Case studies revealed significant qualitative differences in how seemingly similar policies are implemented across countries. Despite similar formal conditionality policies, Finland and the UK differ dramatically in implementation, with Finland adopting a 'human capital' approach focused on skill development versus the UK's 'work first' approach, emphasising short-term employment irrespective of job quality or suitability. These administrative differences may explain divergent outcomes observed across similar welfare regimes. Whilst policy design establishes theoretical incentives and disincentives, administrative practices mediate how these translate into actual experiences for unemployed individuals. 'Street-level' administration of welfare policies creates institutional inertia that may continue to shape behaviour even after formal policy changes (Sadeghi & Terum, 2020).

The research suggests that basic income itself does not inherently incentivise job search activity. Whilst it removes certain disincentives associated with benefit withdrawal and means-testing, this removal alone does not constitute an affirmative incentive to increase work effort. This conclusion challenges how basic income is often framed and evaluated. Many experiments and pilots have been designed primarily to test whether basic income would increase employment through improved financial incentives and reduced administrative burdens. When only small effects are identified, these experiments are often characterised as 'failures'. (De Wispelaere, Halmetoja & Pulkka, 2018; Widerquist, 2018).

Whilst the book examines the potential effects of a basic income on job search activity, it challenges the normative assumption that welfare policies should seek to maximise paid work and argues that job search activities deserve critical examination in light of changing economic and social realities. Any reductions in formal labour market participation following basic income implementation could represent enhanced 'freedom' rather than welfare dependency, allowing individuals to allocate time according to their values rather than purely economic necessity

(Fitzpatrick, 1999; Van Der Veen, 1998; Van Parijs & Vanderborght, 2017; Widerquist, 2013). This might include investing in education, caregiving, community involvement, creative pursuits, or entrepreneurship that traditional labour market metrics fail to capture. This perspective aligns with what Louise Haagh (2008) terms 'developmental freedom', the capacity to make meaningful life choices based on one's values rather than immediate economic pressures.

## Limitations of the Research

Whilst the methodological approach adopted by the book overcomes several limitations that hamper experiments, it does have certain constraints. Firstly, it is a 'snapshot' of life, rather than an analysis of changes over time. The cross-sectional approach captures welfare regimes at a specific moment in time, limiting the ability to assess how institutional arrangements might adapt over time to the introduction of basic income. In addition, the use of time use data, whilst enabling a detailed analysis of behaviour, captures only a slice of life, limited to certain days of the year. This potentially misses out on changes in approach to job search over time.

Secondly, the analysis focuses on the activities of unemployed people, excluding those already in work. The research cannot therefore directly infer the effects of a basic income on those who are currently employed or are completely outside of the labour force. This is particularly relevant to an increasingly fragmented labour market, with the rise of precarious, low paid, jobs with poor conditions. The effects of basic income on this section of the labour force will be incredibly important in determining its overall effects on the labour market.

Thirdly, the analysis focuses on a limited number of countries. Whilst the research covers a variety of welfare regimes, it is limited to European states located in the North, West, and South of the continent. It does not examine the welfare regimes of Eastern Europe or indeed other continents. Inclusion of a larger number of countries would enable a wider range of welfare regimes and institutional contexts to be examined, which may yield different patterns of behaviour.

## Future Research Directions

The limitations identified suggest several promising avenues for future research. The basic income ideal type framework developed in this book could be applied to welfare regimes over time to track evolutionary patterns, revealing whether welfare systems have become more or less aligned with basic income principles in recent decades. With the upcoming release of the 2020 Harmonised European time use data, researchers could examine whether job search patterns have shifted in response to evolving welfare arrangements. This might reveal whether the relationships identified in our analysis remain stable over time or change as welfare regimes and labour markets evolve.

Future research should expand the range of countries and welfare regimes examined to test whether the patterns identified in this book hold across more diverse institutional contexts. Including Eastern European welfare regimes (Aidukaitė, 2010; Fenger, 2007), liberal regimes outside Europe such as Australia and the United States (Esping-Andersen, 1990), welfare states in East Asia (Hort & Kuhnle, 2000; Lee & Ku, 2007; Yang, 2016), and emerging welfare systems in middle-income countries (Seekings, 2005; Dorlach, 2021) would provide a more comprehensive global picture. This expanded diversity would help in determining which findings represent universal patterns across welfare systems and which are specific to certain institutional configurations.

The ideal type framework could be further refined to create more nuanced measures of basic income principles, including more detailed measures of conditionality implementation that capture differences in administrative approach. A particularly promising direction would be developing measures that bridge the gap between formal policy design and actual implementation practices. The framework could also be adapted to examine specific welfare programme types more closely, such as social assistance schemes, which are generally thought to be the closest relations to basic income and may be the easiest to convert.

Future research could examine outcomes beyond job search intensity, such as how welfare arrangements influence the distribution of time between paid work, unpaid work, education, leisure, and community involvement. This broader approach would help capture the multidimensional effects that basic income might have on time allocation and wellbeing, building on existing research in this area (Beaujot & Liu, 2005;

Budlender, 2010; Charmes, 2019). Research should also explore variations within countries across demographic groups, regions, and income distributions, revealing how welfare incentives operate differently for various population segments.

Combining the quantitative approaches with qualitative research could help specify the precise causal mechanisms through which welfare arrangements influence individual decision making. Interviews or ethnographic research with unemployed individuals navigating different welfare systems could reveal how policy designs translate into lived experiences and behavioural responses. This mixed methods approach would help bridge macro level patterns with micro level processes, providing a more complete understanding of how institutional incentives shape individual behaviour.

A crucial area for future research is examining how employers might respond to basic income implementation. Research might explore whether basic income would influence wage levels for low paid work, job quality standards, or employer investments in automation. Would enhanced worker bargaining power lead to improved conditions, or would employers adapt in ways that undermine basic income's potential benefits? These questions require dedicated research examining both theoretical models and empirical evidence from sectors where labour market power dynamics are shifting, which is currently lacking.

## Policy Implications and Closing Reflections

The findings suggest several important considerations for basic income policy development and implementation strategy. Basic income should not be considered a universal solution with predictable effects across all contexts. Instead, implementation strategies must be tailored to specific institutional environments, accounting for existing welfare arrangements, labour market structures, and administrative practices. In Nordic contexts with strong 'human capital' orientations and robust complementary services, basic income might function primarily as an enhancement to existing supports (Haagh, 2011). In welfare contexts like the UK, with 'work first' orientations and limited complementary services, basic income implementation might require more substantial institutional reforms to avoid simply subsidising low wage, precarious employment.

The research highlights the importance of identifying policies that might complement basic income to enhance its positive effects. These include labour market regulation and employment protections, as well as education and training and public services more broadly. Configuration of these complementary policies will vary across contexts, requiring thorough institutional analysis to identify specific gaps or deficiencies in existing frameworks that might limit basic income's effectiveness.

The findings suggest basic income should not be framed primarily as an employment incentive. Its potential benefits lie elsewhere in enhanced financial security, reduced poverty, improved wellbeing, and increased individual autonomy allocations of time use. This supports the work done by basic income experiments where evaluation has broadened beyond narrow labour market metrics to include poverty reduction and income security, wellbeing and health outcomes, time use patterns, empowerment and autonomy, as well as community and social effects (Kangas et al., 2021; McDowell & Ferdosi, 2021);. Future iterations should include a multiple of measures across these domains.

The research suggests that basic income's most significant effects might emerge gradually as institutions and social norms adapt to new arrangements. This long term perspective might include adaptive management approaches with robust monitoring systems, institutional learning mechanisms, consideration of evolving social norms surrounding work and welfare, and regulatory frameworks that respond to potential labour market changes. This book demonstrates that basic income's potential effects depend on complex interactions between policy design, implementation practices, existing institutional contexts, and individual responses. The path from basic income in theory to effective practical implementation requires navigating this complexity with both ambition and humility. By grounding predictions in evidence rather than assumptions, we can develop more realistic expectations and more effective implementation strategies.

For critics concerned about work disincentives, the research offers reassurance that basic income would likely have modest effects on job search activity and labour market participation. For researchers, the methodological framework offers tools to move beyond the limitations of both purely theoretical approaches and geographically constrained experiments. For policymakers, the findings suggest approaching basic income not as a silver bullet but as a potentially transformative policy that requires careful integration within broader institutional frameworks.

As societies continue to face evolving challenges from technological change, labour market precarity and climate change, basic income offers a potential pathway towards more sustainable and equitable social arrangements. By enhancing income security whilst preserving individual autonomy, it might help reconcile economic security with personal freedom in ways that traditional welfare arrangements struggle to achieve. The vision of basic income as enhancing developmental freedom, the capacity to make meaningful life choices aligned with one's values rather than immediate economic pressures, remains powerful. The research suggests this vision is neither utopian nor dystopian but rather a realistic possibility whose realisation depends on thoughtful implementation within supportive institutional frameworks.

The journey from basic income theory to practice continues. This book illuminates important aspects of the path ahead. By grounding analysis in empirical evidence whilst maintaining clarity about basic income's fundamental aims, we can move towards implementation strategies that enhance genuine freedom and financial security for all.

## References

Aidukaitė, J. (2010). Welfare reforms in Central and Eastern Europe: A new type of welfare regime? *Ekonomika, 89*(4), 7–24.

Andersen, N. A., & Larsen, F. (2024). Activation policy: Bruised and battered but still standing. *Policy and Society, 43*(2), 127–140. https://doi.org/10.1093/polsoc/puae013

Ball, E., et al. (2019). *Dealing with welfare conditionality: Implementation and effects*. Policy Press. Retrieved April 22, 2025, from https://books.google.com/books?hl=en&lr=&id=zcaHDwAAQBAJ&oi=fnd&pg=PR1&dq=Welfare+conditionality&ots=ewjV4DF0lp&sig=GiXsnt8QqV7Sy5tryaJpEj97-kU

Beaujot, R., & Liu, J. (2005). Models of time use in paid and unpaid work. *Journal of Family Issues, 26*(7), 924–946. https://doi.org/10.1177/0192513X04273583

Budlender, D. (2010). What do time use studies tell us about unpaid care work? Evidence from seven countries. In *Time use studies and unpaid care work* (pp. 23–67). Routledge. Retrieved April 22, 2025, from https://www.taylorfrancis.com/chapters/edit/10.4324/9780203846148-8/time-use-studies-tell-us-unpaid-care-work-evidence-seven-countries-debbie-budlender

Charmes, J. (2019). *The unpaid care work and the labour market: An analysis of time use data based on the latest world compilation of time-use surveys*. ILO

Geneva. Retrieved April 22, 2025, from https://www.bollettinoadapt.it/wp-content/uploads/2020/01/wcms_732791.pdf

De Wispelaere, J., Halmetoja, A., & Pulkka, V.-V. (2018). The rise (and fall) of the basic income experiment in Finland. In *CESifo forum*. München: ifo Institut–Leibniz-Institut für Wirtschaftsforschung an der ... (pp. 15–19). Retrieved April 22, 2025, from https://www.econstor.eu/bitstream/10419/186082/1/CESifo-Forum-2018-3-3.pdf

Dorlach, T. (2021). The causes of welfare state expansion in democratic MIDDLE-INCOME countries: A literature review. *Social Policy & Administration, 55*(5), 767–783. https://doi.org/10.1111/spol.12658

Esping-Andersen, G. (1990). *The three worlds of welfare capitalism*. Princeton University Press. Retrieved April 22, 2025, from https://books.google.com/books?hl=en&lr=&id=ERCnDwAAQBAJ&oi=fnd&pg=PR8&dq=esping+andersen&ots=0EfqgBd1Qt&sig=1fzL3Snh5oIq8tHHQEAUtM46ZEE

Fenger, M. (2007). Welfare regimes in Central and Eastern Europe: Incorporating post-communist countries in a welfare regime typology. *Contemporary Issues and Ideas in Social Sciences, 3*(2), 1–30.

Fitzpatrick, T. (1999) *Freedom and security: An introduction to the basic income debate*. Springer. Retrieved April 22, 2025, from https://books.google.com/books?hl=en&lr=&id=xeyGDAAAQBAJ&oi=fnd&pg=PP1&dq=Basic+income+AND+Freedom&ots=O3ekwWynC9&sig=8b1vmFbNJ94aHJL6pxSVv5YoiU4

Haagh, L. (2008). Developmental freedom and social order: Rethinking the relation between work and equality. *Journal of Philosophical Economics*, 1(Articles). Retrieved April 22, 2025, from https://jpe.episciences.org/10559

Haagh, L. (2011). Basic income, social democracy and control over time. *Policy & Politics, 39*(1), 43–66. https://doi.org/10.1332/030557311X546316

Hort, S. O., & Kuhnle, S. (2000). The coming of East and South-East Asian welfare states. *Journal of European Social Policy, 10*(2), 162–184. https://doi.org/10.1177/a012488

Jones, K., Wright, S., & Scullion, L. (2024). The impact of welfare conditionality on experiences of job quality. *Work, Employment and Society, 38*(6), 1658–1679. https://doi.org/10.1177/09500170231219677

Kangas, O., et al. (2021). *Experimenting with unconditional basic income: Lessons from the Finnish BI experiment 2017–2018*. Edward Elgar Publishing. Retrieved February 7, 2024, from https://books.google.com/books?hl=en&lr=&id=d3g8EAAAQBAJ&oi=fnd&pg=PR1&dq=Experimenting+with+Unconditional+Basic+Income:+Lessons+from+the+Finnish+BI+...&ots=TOiHW1qqm5&sig=V_cSv1zIVC4jCNSNQxqho7yx8vQ

Lee, Y., & Ku, Y. (2007). East Asian welfare regimes: Testing the hypothesis of the developmental welfare state. *Social Policy & Administration, 41*(2), 197–212. https://doi.org/10.1111/j.1467-9515.2007.00547.x

Mathur, V., Roberts, L., Bezeczky, Z., Lloyd, H., Vallis, D., Sanders, M., ... & Westlake, D. (2025). Basic income for care leavers in Wales pilot evaluation: second annual report, 2024 to 2025.

McDowell, T., & Ferdosi, M. (2021). The impacts of the Ontario basic income pilot: A comparative analysis of the findings from the Hamilton Region. *Basic Income Studies, 16*(2), 209–256. https://doi.org/10.1515/bis-2020-0034

Ragin, C. C. (2004). Turning the tables: How case-oriented research challenges variable-oriented research. In *Rethinking social inquiry: Diverse tools, shared standards* (pp. 123–38).

Reeves, A., & Loopstra, R. (2017). "Set up to fail"? How welfare conditionality undermines citizenship for vulnerable groups. *Social Policy and Society, 16*(2), 327–338.

Riutort, S., Laín, B., & Julià, A. (2023). Basic income at municipal level: Insights from the Barcelona B-MINCOME pilot. *Basic Income Studies, 18*(1), 1–30. https://doi.org/10.1515/bis-2021-0047

Sadeghi, T., & Terum, L. I. (2020). Frontline managers' perceptions and justifications of behavioural conditionality. *Social Policy & Administration, 54*(2), 219–235. https://doi.org/10.1111/spol.12574

Seekings, J. (2005). *Prospects for basic income in developing countries: A comparative analysis of welfare regimes in the South*. Retrieved April 22, 2025, from https://open.uct.ac.za/handle/11427/19413

Van Der Veen, R. J. (1998). Real freedom versus reciprocity: Competing views on the justice of unconditional basic income. *Political Studies, 46*(1), 140–163. https://doi.org/10.1111/1467-9248.00134

Van Parijs, P., & Vanderborght, Y. (2017). Basic income and the freedom to lead a good life. In: *The good life beyond growth* (pp. 153–161). Routledge. Retrieved April 22, 2025, from https://www.taylorfrancis.com/chapters/edit/10.4324/9781315542126-13/basic-income-freedom-lead-good-life-philippe-van-parijs-yannick-vanderborght

Verho, J., Hämäläinen, K., & Kanninen, O. (2022). Removing welfare traps: Employment responses in the Finnish basic income experiment. *American Economic Journal: Economic Policy, 14*(1), 501–522. https://doi.org/10.1257/pol.20200143

Watts, B., & Fitzpatrick, S. (2018). *Welfare conditionality*. Routledge. Retrieved April 22, 2025, from https://www.taylorfrancis.com/books/mono/10.4324/9781315652047/welfare-conditionality-beth-watts-suzanne-fitzpatrick

Widerquist, K. (2005). A failure to communicate: What (if anything) can we learn from the negative income tax experiments? *The Journal of Socio-Economics, 34*(1), 49–81.

Widerquist, K. (2013). *Independence, propertylessness, and basic income: A theory of freedom as the power to say no*. Springer. Retrieved April 21, 2025, from https://books.google.com/books?hl=en&lr=&id=o6yTqTHFnJkC&oi=fnd&pg=PP1&dq=Karl+Widerquist,+March+2013.+Independence,+Propertylessness,+and+Basic+Income:+A+Theory+of+Freedom+as+the+Power+to+Say+No,+New+York:+Palgrave+Macmillan,+&ots=X9aKg4SF38&sig=_9S6yr0z4SaF44zi_-DojvGtWsM
Widerquist, K. (2018). *A critical analysis of basic income experiments for researchers, policymakers, and citizens*. Springer International Publishing. https://doi.org/10.1007/978-3-030-03849-6
Widerquist, K. (2019). The negative income tax experiments of the 1970s. In M. Torry (Ed.), *The Palgrave international handbook of basic income* (pp. 303–318). Springer International Publishing (Exploring the Basic Income Guarantee). https://doi.org/10.1007/978-3-030-23614-4_15
Yang, N. (2016). *Explaining welfare development in East Asia by using set-theoretic methods: East Asia in transition*. PhD Thesis. University of York. Retrieved April 22, 2025, from https://etheses.whiterose.ac.uk/id/eprint/15607/

# Index






S. Watkins, *Basic Income, Work Incentives and Job Search Behaviour*, Exploring the Basic Income Guarantee,
https://doi.org/10.1007/978-3-031-99197-4

The manufacturer's authorised representative in the EU is Springer Nature Customer Service Centre GmbH, Europaplatz 3, 69115 Heidelberg, Germany. If you have any concerns regarding our products, please contact ProductSafety@springernature.com

Printed and bound by CPI Group (UK) Ltd, Croydon, CR0 4YY
30/09/2026
02225507-0001